ANDRE SIMMONS'

"THE SALT FROM THEIR TEARS"

BASED ON TRUE LIFE EVENTS

D1198748

DEDICATION

As a father, writing this book about the story of my daughters was a surreal process that inadvertently resulted in much needed therapy. I am forever grateful to have been blessed with such wonderful daughters; Nadia, Courtnee, Dominique, Chantice, Hakima and Jazmin.

I would also like to give emphasis for a special dedication to two of my daughters Hakima Bell and Dominique S. Simmons, who made her transition to heaven as she passed away in my arms. Dominique's and Hakima's death showed me the greatest gift daughters and fathers can ever share is their love, time and presence with each other. TIMELESS!!!

"THE SALT FROM THEIR TEARS"

BASED ON TRUE LIFE EVENTS

The Salt From Their Tears

INTRODUCTION

The spring of 2020...

"...There is a thin line between sanity and insanity. Sometimes we can barely notice when which is which. For example, yesterday, i was a mentally healthy woman with a healthy and loving family. My psychological and emotional well-being was sound and intact. Today, i would diagnose myself with suffering from a severe and damaging mental illness. I am not stable. My mind is battling itself between sanity and insanity."

Khloe, April and Kiera look at one another with confusion.

"I'm not sure we understand what you're talking about," Khloe said.

"You see, I know who you are but neither of you know who I am. I don't know if you're stupid or just lazy thinkers," Karen replied.

"Daddy was right, this lady acting crazy, y'all," Kiera said nervously.

"What the hell are you talking about?" Khloe asked impatiently.

"Shut the hell up! I ask the questions in here. Now..." Karen pulls out a gun and points it at the sisters. "One of you bitches slept with my husband and that completely ruined my life. So, since you have destroyed my family, I feel it's only fair if I destroy yours. Today, we will all die."

"Oh, my God! You're the wife!" April shouted.

Karen nervously waves the gun aimlessly in the air. She grips the trigger and then points it back and forth at all three of the girls.

"So, which of you dirty little whores want to die first?" Karen frowns sinisterly. "How about I start with the oldest and work my way down, huh?"

Khloe, April and Kiera have scared looks on their faces.

"Look, this gotta be a misunderstanding or something. You got us mixed up with somebody else."

"No, I have the right people who hurt my family and I am about to settle the score."

"I don't know what you need to settle, but it ain't with me. I don't even like men. So, can I go?" Kiera pleaded.

"Really, Kiera?" Khloe snapped.

"Why everybody gotta die?" Kiera cried.

"Look, I slept with the Senator, so I'll deal with the consequences," April looked at Khloe and Kiera and said, "Let my sisters go."

"Aww, look at you. Willing to die for the clan," Karen said sarcastically, "My office. My rules. You destroyed my entire family. Now I'm going to destroy your entire family."

Khloe grabs Kiera and April's hands, "You may kill us. But you can never destroy us or our family, you crazy bitch!"

"Is that right?" Karen holds the gun in the air, "Die!"

Khloe, April and Kiera stand, clutch each other's arms and prepare for Karen to fire the weapon. Karen walks from behind her desk and aims the gun at Khloe. Khloe pushes April and Kiera behind her. When Karen puts her finger on the trigger, I rushed through the door, catching her off guard. I saw the gun in her hand, pointed at my daughters. Although I was seeing it with my own eyes, I still couldn't believe it. It was surreal.

"What the hell are you doing?" I shouted.

"DADDY!" the girls screamed in unison. Karen was surprised. "I tried to spare you the same fate as your homewrecking daughters but...like always, here you are being the good Daddy."

I positioned myself between Karen and the girls, "Things are not as bad as they seem. Put down the gun."

"You don't know what my life is like, Mr. Simms. My husband is gone."

"You're right, you're right," I tried to alleviate the tension by agreeing with Karen. "I don't know. But what I do know is, wherever he is, he is not with one of my girls. I can guarantee you that."

"Ask them!" Karen gestures with her gun for me to ask my girls about her husband. "Ask your precious girls about my husband!"

Without taking my eyes off of Karen, I asked my girls about the Senator, "What uh, what's she talking about, girls?"

"I had an affair with her husband, Daddy. But it was way before we met her," Khloe said.

Karen shouted, "It doesn't matter! You knew he was married!"

"He told me he was getting a divorce! How did I know he was lying? His wife lived in Georgia! He lived in Washington!" Khloe was crying as she was pleading for forgiveness from Karen, me and herself.

"You knew exactly what you were doing," Karen said.

"Look!" I shouted. "She's sorry. I'm sorry. But we need to relax and think about what's happening right now."

"There's nothing to think about. It's over. My marriage. My family. My life. It's over."

"Don't talk like that. You've helped so many people. So many people. You're the best at this. And like you said earlier, everybody wants you to help them and nobody wants to help you. Well, I'm here. I'm here to help you."

"You're here to help your whores!"

"No! No!" I shook my head and then nodded, "Yes, I am, but I'm here to help you, too."

"It's too late. You can't help me, Mr. Simms."

"I can, if you can just help me, to help you. I need you. I need you to help me. I want all of us to walk out that door...together."

"I'm sorry." Karen wiped her eyes with the hand that was holding the gun and then she shook her head, no. "We're not leaving. None of us are."

"Well, let my daughters go and you and I can stay here and talk. We can talk as long as you want. For as long as it takes."

"They are the ones who did this to me! They are going to die with me!" Karen shouted.

"No, they're not. You're not going to hurt them. You wanna know why? Because you know they're not responsible for your husband. Your husband is responsible for hurting you. Come on, you know this. Still, it's never too late." I tried to switch my negotiation tactic to reinforcing the possibility that Karen's marriage could be saved, and I received the shock of my life. "Maybe if you all talked, get counseling, who knows? Maybe you can salvage your marriage."

"It's too late."

"Only if you think it's too late. You all have a history. You have children. It's never too…"

Karen yelled at me while I was in mid-sentence, "IT'S TOO GOTDAM LATE!"

"OK! OK! OK! Calm down," While Karen was distracted with her frustration, I started to move slowly towards the door as I continued to talk. Slowly pushing my daughters towards that door. "I'm just looking at things from all angles."

Finally, the girls were at the door and I stood between them and Karen. Khloe inconspicuously reached for the doorknob as Karen continued to talk to me.

"What kind of a person can save everyone but herself?"

"This is not your fault, Karen," I said. "Don't go blaming yourself. It's not your fault! It's not the girls' fault! The Senator did this, and he has to fix it."

"It's too late!" Karen shouted again.

I looked back at Khloe and she looked at me. I nodded, cluing her to get ready to make her move. I was nervous. The girls were scared. I had my weapon inside the waist of my pants, so I would have to snatch my pistol out simultaneously as the girls ran outside. I didn't want to hurt Karen, I had grown quite fond of her. She had helped me when I needed help most and I was indebted to her. But we were at a crossroad of the survival of the fittest and it was either Karen or my girls.

"Why is it too late?" I tried one more attempt to reason.

I had no more negotiation tactics. No more pleading. No more answers. It was time for me to get my daughters out of that potentially deadly situation. I didn't care what happened to me.

I didn't want to die but if it meant saving my daughters, I was willing to die in an instant. I just wanted them safe.

Time was up! The moment of truth had arrived. I looked over to Khloe and then I looked into the eyes of Kiera and April. I could see and feel their fear through the tears flowing from all of their eyes. The salt from their tears began to rain down upon my heart and I realized that this was the moment I would purify those tears and rectify my past. My life for their lives. My mind was swirling. My heart was racing. As I reached for my weapon, Karen replied to my question.

"He's dead," Karen mumbled.

I stopped motioning for my weapon and the girls stopped reaching for the door, as we tried to process what we had just heard.

"What?" I said in disbelief.

"It's too late because he's dead."

"What…what are you saying?"

"He's gone," Karen started to raise her gun and I reached for mine. "My husband is dead. I killed him."

"I beg you, please, put that weapon down and let's talk this out!"

"It's too late." Karen lowered her gun and I began to relax, but it was only for a moment.

Suddenly, Karen raised her gun, forcing me once again to pull my weapon. Karen pointed her gun at me, and I pointed my gun at her, while pushing my girls out of the door. She had a clear shot at my chest but instead of firing, she spread a sad grin across her face and then continued to raise the gun.

"NOOOOOOOOOOOOO!" I screamed, as she pulled the trigger.

The Salt From Their Tears

TABLE OF CONTENTS

CHAPTER ONE

The summer of 2001...

G ood afternoon, Mr. Simms."

"Good afternoon, Dr. Turner."

"Thank you for coming today. Let me first explain what I do, and how I can help. Family therapy is a form of psychotherapy that seeks to reduce distress and conflict by improving the systems of interactions between family members. While family therapists often seek to have all family members who are affected by the problem in the room, that is not always possible or necessary. As in your case.

"Family therapy is defined as anyone who plays a long-term supportive role in one's life, which may not mean blood relations, or even family members, who live in the same household. Family relationships are viewed as important for good mental health, regardless of whether all family members are participating in the therapy or not. It is an ideal counseling method for helping family members adjust to another immediate family member who may be struggling with an addiction, medical issue or mental health diagnosis. It is also recommended for improving communication and reducing conflict. OK, so far?"

"Yes."

On my first visit to Dr. Turner's office, I was apprehensive, nervous and uncomfortable. Like most black men, I saw therapy as a mental illness or being mentally weak, and not as treatment. Dr. Turner's initial bombardment of questions did nothing to enhance my comfort level. But my purpose for being there superseded my fearful vulnerability of openly expressing my emotions to a complete stranger. Comfortable or not, I was sitting in her office and I was at the point of no return. I had mixed emotions as I sat and listened to her speak.

"Everyone has a specific perspective on what they think their issue is, and who or what, is the source. More times than not, they are correct in their assumption. Nevertheless, whether it's work related, family, friend or even a stranger, we need to find the source and then find a possible resolution. I'm here to create positive changes as rapidly as possible without making you feel rushed.

"To begin, I have a few introductory questions for you to determine your starting point." Dr. Turner paused momentarily and then continued to speak. "Have you ever received counseling before? If you have, was it effective? If so, were the results long-term or short-term? Was it one session, two sessions, or approximately how many, if you can remember?"

"This is my first time ever receiving counseling."

"Thank you. From your perspective, please explain to me the primary cause of your issue?"

"Uh, yeah," I said reluctantly. "I'm a father. I have three daughters that I raised since they were in their teens. It's becoming a bit overwhelming, and I need to deal with my absence in their lives so that I can deal with them dealing with my absence in their lives. I want to make sure that they can lead productive and constructive lives."

"It appears that you have thought about this for a while and you know exactly what issues you would like to discuss. That's good. There will be times when you will feel vulnerable, exposed, too transparent. Sometimes you may even feel that you are offering too much information. But you won't. The more you express yourself, the more we can determine how to best resolve your issues."

"Thank you," I replied. "As I said, I have three daughters, Khloe, Kiera and April. I love my daughters more than life itself. I can't even explain how much I love them. And when you love something the way you love your child, it makes you feel vulnerable because you want to protect them every second of every day. But we know that's impossible. No matter how much we try, we can't protect our children from everything."

"Apparently, your daughters are a major priority in your life, and you are willing to do what's necessary to assure that they receive all of the attention and care needed to prepare them for life. I commend you for having the courage to unselfishly put the needs of your children before your own apprehensions of coming here. It's not easy to sit in front of someone and tell them intimate and private details of your life."

"I appreciate that, Dr. Turner."

"We are going to discuss each and every one of your children, but before we delve into their lives, I would like for you to tell me about you, your upbringing, and your background."

"I may need a little encouraging."

"That's why you're here, Mr. Simms. To talk about where you came from so that we can understand why you are here, to get you where you need to be. I cannot do that without your help. Do you understand me?"

"Yes. I suppose so."

"Don't worry. We'll go at your pace and we'll discuss whatever you feel comfortable with. If you would rather start with your children, that's perfectly fine."

"Where do you want me to start?"

"From the beginning, Mr. Simms."

"OK," I said. "I'm a big boy, so…I was born in Chicago, Illinois in 1965…"

—

The headlines of the current affairs of 1965 were "The assassination of Malcolm X," "Bloody Sunday in Selma, Alabama," "The first American combat troops arrive in Vietnam," "My Fair Lady wins eight Academy Awards," "President Johnson signs the Voting Rights Act," "A Charlie Brown Christmas debuts" and I was born on July, 11th.

I was born on the south side of Chicago; an area infested with gangs, pimps, prostitutes, and stick up kids. Chicago was the home of an abundance of housing developments. These housing districts were infamously and frightfully known as the Projects. I have lived in Robert Taylor Homes, Altgeld Gardens, and Ida B. Wells. When you are in a low-income or socioeconomic class, it is normal for families to drift from project to project.

I never knew my biological father. My older siblings' father served as my father figure. He was married to my mother and I am still unclear on all of the facts, but at some point, they divorced, I was born and then they somehow reconciled. He took us in and accepted me as his own. He made sure that my older siblings did not treat me as a half-brother. We were one unified family. We were poor but we were happy. My stepfather was a good man who provided the best he could on his modest salary, but he could not support five children and a wife. I was still young, so my mother was a stay-at-home mom who would do small jobs, but she could not contribute much to the household income.

My Auntie, my stepfather's sister, stepped in and let my two older siblings move in with her. This allowed us the opportunity to have space and live only slightly below the poverty line, whereas before, we could not even see the poverty line. Our stability was short lived because my Auntie relocated to New York City and we were back to being a seven-member family living in a five-room apartment; two bedrooms, one bathroom, one kitchen and a living room.

While coming home from work one night, my stepfather was shot and killed in front of our apartment building. The assailant wasn't prosecuted or caught. Rumors around the neighborhood was that he owed a loan shark money and did not pay his debt. His death shattered the foundation of our family. My mother no longer had the provider and protector she needed. My older brother no longer had the role model to keep him from the waiting arms of the streets. My sisters no longer had the constant love and affection from the first man they ever loved. I no longer had the familiar presence of a structured family unit.

We started to see the crumbling of our family when my brother was arrested for armed robbery. He was ten years older than me and he would take me on some of his criminal capers. I was six-years-old when he took me on a run to rob a corner store. He figured no one would suspect a robbery if he was with a child. I did not know what was happening at the time, everything simply seemed chaotic. He ran and my little six-year-old legs ran as fast as they could to keep up with him. After that, he was in and out of juvenile facilities more than he was at home. I wanted to be like him.

My sisters and I started to skip school and the truant officers contacted the state authorities to investigate our home environment. They found my mother and our home to be unfit and my sisters and I were placed in foster care. We were placed in different homes and did not see, or visit, one another. We ran away often trying to find our mother, and each other, but to no avail. I ended up homeless and in detention centers for running away and stealing. Eventually, my mother managed to pull herself together and convince the courts that she was fit to re-establish custody of us. Then we moved into the luxurious Cabrini-Green Estates.

As I mentioned, I was raised in several housing projects. Of them all, Cabrini-Green was the most notorious, not just in the city of Chicago, but in all of the United States. Cabrini-Green suffered decades of poverty and violence which eventually left it dilapidated and uninhabitable. It has since been demolished and the residents have been relocated to other neighborhoods. Some were fortunate enough to move into brand new condos and other living areas. Unfortunately, some became homeless and were left to fend for themselves.

The notoriety of Cabrini-Green brought attention that led the projects to the small and big screen. The movie "Candyman" was filmed in Cabrini-Green. The classic movie "Cooley High" was also filmed in the vicinity of the Cabrini-Green projects. The popular show "Good Times" was based on the Cabrini-Green projects. What the television show did not tell were the stories of civilian snipers on rooftops shooting at police officers. Cabrini-Green was so violent, that after one murder, the police decided it was best to let the Project police its own crimes because it was too dangerous for the officers. That murder was the first time I ever saw a dead body.

My mother and I were going to get on the elevator and when it opened a gang of boys ran out. They were pulling on a kid who they had beaten but he was still alive. I was in complete and utter shock. My mother pulled me to the side to let them pass. We could see the red and blue lights flashing from outside. The boys yelled through the door to the officers. It was the leader. His name was Pop.

"Hey!" Pop yelled. "We 'bout to come out. Back up or I'mma put a hot one in this fool!"

"Let him go, Pop," Mama cried. "You're about to take his life and ruin yours. It ain't worth it. Turn yourself in."

"This fool tried to rob us and now they comin' here to get us? They need to let the streets handle the streets."

The fool that Pop and his gang had beaten was an old school rival named Lang, who was trying to take over their building. They had set him up and were going to make sure he knew whose territory it was.

"You boys are already in trouble, son. Turn yourself in."

"I ain't goin' to jail for nobody. If they kill me, they kill me. We can shoot it out right now."

Pop stood between Lang and freedom. As Pop was talking to my mother, Lang saw that he was distracted and lunged at him to try to make an escape. Pop pointed the gun at Lang and fired several shots. Lang instantly fell to the floor. My mother pulled me to her and covered me up as the gunshots were fired. I started to cry as I looked around and saw Lang's lifeless body lying on the floor.

When the police officers heard the gunshots, they rushed the door. They were met with a flurry of gunshots and a few of them were hit. After that day, Pop and every member of his crew who was with him in that lobby went to jail. The Chicago Police Department, or as we referred to them, the CPD, only came around sparingly, and my mother started to slip into a deep depression from the trauma. I, on the other hand, though frightened by the violence, found the scenario somewhat exciting and thrilling.

Sometimes on the Fourth of July weekend, or during the New Year's celebration, gang members would shoot guns in the air with no thought of harm or injury to others. It was a very dangerous situation. My mother never let us leave the apartment on those holidays. On one particular Fourth of July celebration, Mama was in a more pleasant than normal mood and she allowed us to go outside. There were the typical gunshots but nothing excessive. Everybody was having a good time.

My mother would come to our window and look down on us to make sure everything was fine with us. As we were engrossed in our rare outdoor playtime, my mother noticed strange cars circling the block. It could have been visitors for another family looking for parking or making sure they had the right building, but my mother's instinctive fear, or some may call it traumatic paranoia, kicked in and she yelled for us to come upstairs.

We were confused, but we did as our mother told us. As soon as we stepped in our apartment, it sounded like a Vietnam battlefield outside. My mother pulled all of us to the floor and covered us with her body.

"Get down! Get down! Get down!" Mama yelled.

We scrambled across the floor dodging and ducking bullets my mother tried her best to shield from as many of us as possible. We made it to the bathroom where she put us in the tub and on the side of the toilet where the commode could block bullets. She put herself between us and the direction that the bullets were being fired and we waited impatiently for the gunfire to stop. After the shots ceased, my mother did a body check on all of us to make sure we were unharmed.

"Oh, God," Mama cried, as one by one, she hugged us. "You OK, baby?

"Yes, ma'am," we answered.

"Thank You, Lord, thank You," Mama rocked back and forth. "I can't take it no mo'. I just can't take it."

My home environment gradually became unstable and it began to noticeably take its toll on my mother. Day by day, I could see her strength and faith start to erode. At one point, alcohol was not allowed in our home. But as the conditions around us worsened, my mother started to rely more and more on alcohol to help her get through the days to go to work, then through the nights to help her sleep, and finally to get up to go back to work.

Although my mother's mental condition weakened because of the projects, my siblings and I became immune to our circumstances. It was the only life we knew. Under normal circumstances and a clear mental state, my mother was a lovely woman who cared deeply for her children. Nevertheless, she had her demons. The most critical for our family was her alcohol addiction. There were times when she was under the influence that she would become a totally different person; a terrifying and violent person.

—

We moved from the second floor to the seventh floor of Cabrini-Green, and we always had a big fence. This fence was well-known for people jumping over it to escape to safety, or for dead bodies being thrown over it to dispose of them. For some of us, the projects became somewhat like a prison, because it trapped us inside with some of the most dangerous people in the city. As I reflect back on those times growing up in the projects, I recall the days as always being gloomy and dark, even when the sun was shining. It was a very difficult time for me.

A couple of pleasant memories are of myself riding in a little red wagon, going back and forth in front of my neighbors' houses. Meanwhile, my mother would be on the inside of our apartment with the door open drinking beer with one of her friends. When she was sober, she was a gentle and loving soul. In regards to my mother and her friends socializing, what looked like fun to me was actually a group of enabling drunken women with no help to recovery and no way out of the condition causing them to drink. However, my mother was what we called a functioning alcoholic. She drank as much as she could and worked as much as she could. That left my siblings and me a lot of time with no parental supervision.

Not having a male role model to provide a sense of direction, I was lost and followed the popular boys in the projects. Unfortunately, the popular boys were gang members and criminals.

"Hey, 'Dre?" Moon, a notorious gang leader, said as he called me over to his car. "Come 'mere, lil' man. Let me holla at you."

I was excited that Moon had taken the time to acknowledge me. As far as I knew, he did not even know I existed. All of the Project kids looked up to Moon. He was an idol. He had lots of money, lots of cars and lots of girls. All the things that every neighborhood boy wanted, including me.

"Hey, Moon," I said excitedly, "you want me?"

"Yeah, you wanna job?"

"Yeah, doing what?"

"I need you to just stand over there for me," Moon pointed to the corner of the block. "Look, lil' man, if you see the cops coming down the street, either way, I want you to run inside and tell Big Run."

Big Run was actually a very little man. Everybody knew him from panhandling and selling miscellaneous stuff on the block. Most of the stuff he sold was stolen from the neighbors of the people who were buying it. Quite often, when some of the victims saw their neighbors with their stolen items, they would assume Big Run's customers were the perpetrators who ripped them off. It was not surprising when the mistaken identity would lead to violent retaliation. All the while, Big Run stayed above the fray.

"OK, that's all I gotta do?" I asked.

"Yeah," Moon assured me. "Can you handle that?"

"Yeah," I replied.

"You ain't scared or nothin', are you?"

"Naw."

"You sure? I can't have no cowards working for me, man. You gotta be a man."

"I'm a man. I can do it."

Like so many others in my projects, I was eleven years old and I was declaring myself to be a man. When you declared yourself as a man, the streets expected for you to be a man and it did not give a damn if you were a grown man or a brand-new baby. If you were expected to do a job, you better do it or suffer the consequences.

"How long do I have to stand over there?" I asked.

"Until I say you can go home."

"OK, but my mama said I have to be in the house before it get dark."

"Really," Moon laughed out loud. "You don't want no job, lil' man, you still a kid."

"I ain't no kid. I can stay out here as long as I want."

"Boy, get yo' little ass in the house. You don't wanna make no money."

"Yeah, I do," I pleaded. "Come on, Moon. I don't care what my mama say. I wanna make some money."

"Look-a-here. If you do a good job, I'mma take care of you. You can help yo' mama out with y'all bills. I'm tellin' you, yo' mama will respect you after this."

"She will?"

"Yeah."

"How much do I get paid?"

"You get paid whatever I pay you, now get yo' little ass over there and man that corner before I change my mind."

"OK," I quickly ran over to the corner and posted up.

Moon and his entourage sat in their car and watched carefully as several different people walked to and from the car. At that time, I did not know the reason why there were so many people surrounding Moon's car. Half were there to buy drugs and the other half were there to protect Moon while he was selling the drugs.

It was beginning to get dark and I knew that my mother would be coming home from work soon. No matter what I told Moon, I did not want to be standing on that corner when my mother came home.

I wondered when Moon was going to tell me that I could go home. I had been standing on the corner for approximately an hour with no incident and I was ready to go. As I looked to my left, I saw a Chicago Police Department patrol car cruising down the street. I panicked. I wanted to run immediately and into the building and tell Big Run the cops were coming, but they were too close. I thought that if they saw me run, it would clue them that something was happening so I casually walked towards the building.

I glanced over to Moon's car and made eye contact with him. He looked at me, and I used a hand signal pointing towards the direction of the upcoming patrol car to tip him off. He nodded and I continued towards the building. When I was out of sight of the cops, I ran into the building screaming to Big Run.

"The cops are coming, Big Run!" I yelled.

"Oh, shit!" Big Run screamed nervously. "Shut it down! Shut it down!"

People started to scatter all over the place. I was right there in the middle of the chaos. I did not know which way to run so I sat frozen in a catatonic state of fear. Then out of nowhere, I felt the back of my shirt being snatched and I was off of my feet. I could not see who had grabbed me, I only knew that we were moving and moving fast.

Moon had the elevator blocked off and no one could go up or down until he had finished his business. His business was interrupted by the CPD but he had not given clearance to operate the elevators. That meant nobody but Moon's business associates should have been on the first floor. Except my mother, of course.

"What the hell you doin' down here, boy?" my mother said as she pushed the elevator button.

"I was tryin' to get upstairs."

"What you doin' down here in the first place?" my mother screamed. "You supposed to have yo' ass upstairs in that apartment."

"I was coming to meet you, Mama."

"I don't need you to meet me," Mama said, as we stepped into the elevator. "I got something for you to meet when we get in this apartment."

Mama was mad at everybody. As soon as she stepped one foot into our apartment she started yelling and screaming.

"FELICIA! TRACY! STACY!" Mama screamed. "BRING Y'ALL ASSES HERE RIGHT NOW!"

My sisters ran out of the bedroom that the three of them shared. My sisters and I were all two years apart. My oldest sister, Felicia, was seventeen. My sister Tracy was fifteen. My sister Stacy was thirteen. I had an older brother, Christopher, who was eighteen and serving time for armed robbery. He was a gang member himself. Mama tried everything she could to try to steer him from the streets, but he had too many influences. That left my older sisters to guide and protect me. For the most part, they did a pretty good job. But there was only so much they could do.

"You called us, Mama?" Felicia said, as Tracy and Stacy stood slightly behind her. Felicia was our second mother. She was tough. She knew how to handle the gangs and how to stay away from them. She was not afraid of them because she grew up with them.

"How come y'all let this boy outside?"

"We didn't let him outside, Mama. He never came home from school," Felicia looked at me and rolled her eyes.

"I come home from a hard day's work to this?"

"It wasn't our fault, Mama. Andre know he supposed to come in this house when he get outta' school."

"I don't care! You the oldest. Make sure he get in here. Y'all in here playin' around and that boy could be somewhere dead."

"Mama, we didn't know where he was and Moon had put our building on lockdown. What was we supposed to do?" Tracy replied. Tracy was the middle girl and loaded with attitude. She had a smart mouth which would sometime get her in trouble with my mother.

"I don't care who had the building on what. Do what I tell you to do!" Mama screamed.

"We sorry, Mama," Stacy spoke softly. Stacy was soft-spoken. She was an excellent student and never gave my mother trouble. She tended to have a calming effect on my mother.

"Sorry is not going to save your life. Do what I tell you to do and you will live to get the hell up outta' here. Do y'all understand me?"

"Yes, ma'am," my sisters said in unison.

While my mother was scolding my sisters for not knowing where I had been after school, I sat on the couch trying to avoid her wrath. My mother walked to her bedroom, still fussing to my sisters. I took a deep sigh and finally relaxed. As long as my mother did not know what happened that day, I would live to see another day. But...

"DREEEEEE?" Mama yelled. "Bring yo' ass in here."

I slow-walked to my mother's bedroom. Waiting for me was a long switch that we called "Killa." Killa and I had met on quite a few occasions and he had beat my ass every single time. As soon as I saw that switch in mother's hand I began to cry.

"Mama, I won't do it no more," I cried.

"Yes, you will because you told me that the last time."

My mother spanked me very soundly that night. I could feel her pain, fear and disappointment with every swat. I went to bed that night thinking of how I would face Moon the next time I saw him. He owed me money. I really did not care about the money at that point. It was not as if I could make him pay me anyway. After that beating I took that night, all that I wanted to do was come home after school and watch cartoons like every other child my age.

—

"How did you feel after your mother spanked you?" Dr. Turner asked.

"I wanted to run away. I wanted to get out of there because I knew the next day was going to be more of the same."

We talked more about my feelings on the events of that night until Dr. Turner looked at her watch and then smiled, "I see that we have exceeded our time, but that is a good thing. I will have my secretary schedule you for your next session. I look forward to seeing you again, Mr. Simms."

I shook Dr. Turner's hand and exited her office. My first session was everything, and nothing, as I expected. Surprisingly, I was looking forward to my next visit.

CHAPTER TWO

The summer of 2011...

On my second visit to Dr. Turner, I was still slightly apprehensive, but I felt more comfortable than I did on the first visit. She wanted to pick up exactly where we left off, so we greeted one another and then transitioned directly into therapy.

"How are you, Mr. Simms?" Dr. Turner asked.

"I'm OK, how are you?"

"I'm great," Dr. Turner looked at her laptop and then raised her head and started talking. "So, at our last session, you left off where you were disciplined by your mother for not going home after school. Did you return to the gang, or did you follow your mother's rules and go home after school?"

"Unfortunately, no." I responded firmly.

—

The next day, my plan was to go straight upstairs to our apartment and stay out of trouble. However, Moon was parked outside of our building again. As I tried to walk past him, he called me over to his car again.

"Hey, lil' man?" Moon yelled. "Bring yo' little ass here."

I ran over to Moon's car, which was filled with young men sitting with guns in their hands as well as on their laps. Big Run was sitting in the front passenger seat.

"Hey, Moon?"

"Good lookin' out yesterday. You came through for me."

"Thanks."

"I like that. I'mma have more work for you."

"Thanks."

"Here you go," Moon handed me a one-hundred-dollar bill.

"Yoooooooo'," I said with amazement. "I can keep this?"

"Yeah, lil' man," Moon chuckled. "That's yours."

"I ain't never had this much money before in my life."

"Look, there's a lot more where that came from. You do good work and you get paid good money. They don't teach you that in school but that's how it is out here in the streets."

"OK."

"Look, though," Moon looked around. "You bet' not tell nobody where you got that money from, or that you work for me. If you do, you know what's gon' happen, don't you?"

"Yeah," I spoke softly.

"You do? What's gon' happen?"

"You gon' kill me."

"Nah, lil' man," Moon laughed. "I ain't gon' kill you. I ain't a killa', but I will do something very, very, very, ve-ry bad to yo' mama and yo' sisters if I find out you puttin' my business in the streets. You see what I'm saying?"

"I ain't gon' tell nobody nothin'," I was so nervous I was shaking in my shoes.

"Dre?" Felicia shouted from the front of our building.

I turned around and looked at her and shouted back, "What you want?"

"Get in here befo' you get in trouble."

"Day-um," Moon said. "Who dat is?"

"Oh, that's just my sister?"

"Is that Felicia?" Big Run asked.

"Yeah." I answered.

"Man, yo' sister fine as hell," Moon sat up and looked through the windshield to get a closer look. "I think I know her. I went to high school with her. Her name Tracy ain't it?"

"Naw, Tracy is my other sister. That's my oldest sister right there," I said, pointing at Felicia. "Her name is Felicia."

"Hey, lil' man, I need to holla at yo' sister."

I knew that Moon was not my sister's type of guy. She was attracted to scholarly or academic nerds, not street thugs.

"My mama don't let her date nobody."

"They mama kinda' strict on all them girls, Moon."

"I don't care what they mama say. This is my Projects. I run Cabrini-Green and I get what I want, nigga. You got somethin' to say about that?"

"Naw, Moon, I'm just sayin'. She don't mess with our type of niggas, man."

"Our type of nigga?" Moon looked at all of the guys in the backseat. "This nigga think he me. You ain't me, nigga. You just wanna be me."

"It ain't even like that, Moon."

"It is like that, punk. You been trying to move in on me since day one."

"What are you talking about, Moon? I raised yo' ass. I brought you up in the streets. I made you who you is, nigga."

"Yeah, that's the problem. Yo' old ass think I owe you something. I don't owe you shit, nigga. Be glad you sittin' in the front seat with me," Moon's sarcasm instantly turned to rage. "Naw, hell, naw. Be glad you even sittin' in the same car with me."

"DRE!" Felicia yelled louder. "Come 'mere, right now befo' I tell Mama on you."

"Here I come!" I yelled back. "I gotta' go, Moon."

"Hold on a second. Let me finish with this fool first. Then I'mma go talk to yo' sister. Tell her to hold on for a minute."

"OK," I turned and ran over to Felicia.

"What are you doin' over there talkin' to Moon?" Felicia asked.

"He just wanted to holla at me for a minute."

"Holla at you? Why you talkin' like that?"

"'Cause that's how we talk in the streets."

"You ain't from no streets. You from the ghetto. Now let's go upstairs."

"Moon said he wanna' talk to you for a minute."

"I'm not talkin' to that fool."

"You got to."

"What you mean, I got to? I ain't gotta' do shit."

"Hey, hey, girl?" Moon shouted through the passenger window as he leaned across Big Run. "Come here for a minute."

"I can't."

"Why not?"

"'Cause I gotta' do somethin'."

"Hey, Felicia," Big Run shouted, "It's cool. He just wanna' talk to you for a second."

"Then tell him to come to me."

Big Run and Moon talk amongst themselves momentarily. Moon leans across Big Run again and yells out of the window to Felicia.

"Meet me halfway," Moon yelled.

"Naw, you want me. You come to me."

I started to get nervous, thinking that Moon would get angry and explode on my sister like I had just seen him do to Big Run.

"Yo, hold on." Moon chatted with Big Run and the guys in the car for a minute while Felicia impatiently waited. Then he got out of the car and headed towards Felicia.

"'Sup, babygirl."

"My name is Felicia."

"Hey Felicia, I'm Moon."

"I know who you are."

"You gotta' man?"

"Yup."

"He live in Cabrini-Green?"

"Naw. He live on the eastside."

"Oh, you got one of those eastside niggas, huh?" Moon joked.

"Yup."

"Them niggas weak."

"At least he got a real job and gettin' an education and not sittin' in the car with a bunch of hard legs selling drugs."

"You know who you talkin' to, babygirl?"

"I ain't scared of you, Moon."

"You better watch yo' mouth. I can be your best friend or your worst nightmare, so check yourself."

"Check yourself. This my mouth and I can say whatever I wanna' say."

"Yeeeeeah," Moon laughed as he looked Felicia up and down. "Tough, huh? I like that shit."

"Look, we gotta' go."

"I'mma get back with you, OK?"

"OK, I gotta' go," Felicia turned to me. "Let's go."

I admired how Felicia stood up to Moon. She did not appear to be afraid of him at all. As soon as we walked into the building, Felicia chewed my ass out royally.

"What's wrong with you, boy?" Felicia snapped.

"What you talkin' 'bout?"

"What are you doin' goin' up to Moon's car talkin' to him like that?"

"We was jus' talkin'."

"He sell drugs and he's in a gang. Why are you hanging with him when you know what Mama went through with Chris?"

"I told you we was just talking," I turned the situation around by asking Felicia why she was talking to Moon. "You talkin' about me? Why you talkin' to him?"

"I was just tryin' to be nice to that fool. He ain't my type."

"Man, whatever."

After we entered the apartment, I went straight to my bedroom and hid my money under my mattress. That mattress would infamously become my personal savings and loan bank.

—

Over the next few weeks, Moon kept putting me on that corner and I kept making that money. He started to pay me more and more and asked me to do more work for him, like becoming a runner. In a month's time, I had over two thousand dollars hidden in my room. Can you imagine that? An eleven-year-old resident of Cabrini-Green having two thousand dollars? That was more than the savings account balance of ten different families. It was a bittersweet feeling because I could not spend the money without my mother knowing it. If my mother had ever found out I was getting money from Moon, she would kill me.

While I was working the Projects for Moon, Felicia had flat out told him that he was not her type. So, to spite her, he went after my sister Tracy. Tracy was more influenced by Moon's money and popularity. That relationship would come to a sudden and tragic halt.

"Lil' Man, go get yo' sister for me," Moon told me.

"OK," I said running towards the building.

"Hold it. Hold it," Moon shouted, "Come 'mere, boy."

I walked back to Moon's car and he told me, "tell her to meet me at the penthouse in about five minutes."

I ran back over to Tracy and told her what Moon had said, "Moon said meet him at the penthouse in five minutes."

"OK," Tracy looked towards Moon's car and waved at him. "Tell Felicia I went to the store."

"OK," I said.

Next thing I knew, Tracy was sneaking into Moon's penthouse, which was a few apartments he had taken over and combined into one large, massive living space. For Cabrini-Green, Moon's penthouse was like a five-star hotel suite. Unfortunately for Tracy, Felicia was already on her way down to check on us.

"Where's Tracy?" Felicia asked.

"She left," I said.

"And went where?"

"I don't know."

"So Tracy was just out here and then just all of a sudden disappeared?"

"All I know is, I don't know where she went."

"Well, you better go find her right now or I'm telling Mama."

"OK," I sighed heavily. "She went to the penthouse."

"To meet Moon?"

"Yeah."

"She is out of her rabid mind," Felicia snapped as she stomped towards the penthouse building.

"You want me to come with you?"

"No. Get yo' little ass upstairs in that apartment." I was terrified of my mother and afraid of Moon, but there was something psychotic about Felicia that put the fear of God in me.

Felicia entered Moon's building, walking past his soldiers like she owned the place. She grew up with most of them, so they gave her respect. They also knew that she was my brother Chris' little sister, and if they harmed her, they would have to deal with him when he was released from prison. The biggest protection Felicia had at her disposal, and I truly believe she knew it and used it to her advantage, was the deep affinity that Moon had for her.

Big Run and another soldier, Dice, were sitting outside the front door of the penthouse when Felicia charged the door. To put is simply, Dice was a cold and ruthless hitman. He would kill his mother without blinking his eye, if Moon gave him the command. He felt that Moon and his gang were the only love he ever received, and he considered them family. When Dice saw Felicia coming towards them, he jumped up and pulled out his pistol pointing it at her. Felicia stopped in her tracks in frozen fear.

"Whoa. Whoa. Whoa." Big Run grabbed the gun out of Dice's hand and then looked at Felicia. "What's happenin', Felicia?"

"I came for my sister."

"She busy right now."

"Tell my sister to come 'mere."

"I told you she's busy right now, Felicia, now go on before you piss Moon off."

"I ain't goin' nowhere until my sister come out of there."

"Damn man," Big Run opens the door. "Hold on, Felicia. I'll be right back."

Big Run disappeared behind the door and Felicia and Dice were left standing face to face in a fierce stare down. Dice playfully pointed his gun at Felicia and smiled.

"I ain't scared of no gun," Felicia rolled her eyes.

"You were scared when I was about to pop yo'

ass.""Why you talkin' to a girl like that?"

"I don't care what you are. If you mess with my family. I mess with you."

"Why though?"

"Why though, what?"

"Why y'all gotta' kill up us? We all the same people trying to make it out the ghetto and y'all bringing in y'all drugs and violence and killin' everybody. We tryin' to survive and y'all fools keep actin' crazy."

"Move then," Dice snarled.

"Let me tell you something…"

Big Run opened the door as Felicia was about to explode, "She busy right now."

"So, you sayin' he not gon' let my sister out?"

"She doesn't wanna' come out."

Felicia looked back and forth at Dice and Big Run. Dice smiled and Big Run hunched his shoulders.

"A'ight then," Felicia stormed out the penthouse and came back home.

I heard her come through the door. Everybody heard her come through the door because of how loud she slammed it. I do not recall ever seeing her that angry. But if you thought Felicia was angry? All hell broke loose when my mother came home and realized that Tracy was not there.

"Where's Tracy?" Mama asked.

I closed my door as tight as I could and covered my ears. I knew that my mother was going to erupt, and I wanted no part of it. To my surprise, it was silent. I slightly opened my door and peeked out, and no one was in sight. I walked into our living room and Mama and Felicia were gone. The door was ajar, so I closed and locked it. I sat on the couch and folded my arms. Stacy walked out of my sisters' bedroom, half asleep, and sat next to me. She did not say anything. She wrapped her arms around me and laid my head on her chest. She kissed me on my forehead, and eventually I drifted into sleep.

Meanwhile, my mother and Felicia had returned to the penthouse to get Tracy. Felicia led the way as they approached Big Run and Dice. Big Run sighed and shook his head because he knew what he was about to face with those two ladies.

"Aw, hell naw," Big Run nudged Dice.

"What?"

"Here they come again," Big Run pointed at Mama and Felicia.

"Yooo, we gotta put these hoes on their back, bruh," Dice said.

"Man, that's Ms. Simms, we can't touch her."

"Ain't nobody untouchable. Nobody!"

"Nigga, we don't want them problems."

"Go get my sister." Felicia snapped.

"You heard her," Mama said, as she put her hand on her hips.

"Ms. Simms, look, you know y'all can't be doing this, like this," Big Run tried to alleviate the situation.

"Open that dam' do' and go get my baby," Mama pulled out a gun and pointed it at Big Run and then pointed it at Dice. "And you sit yo' black ass right there and don't move a muscle."

"You better be glad you got that gun," Dice snarled.

"Look boy, I'm nervous. I need a drank. My eyes twitchin' and my hand is shakin' like a sonofabitch. You better be glad I don't pull this trigger."

Felicia opens the door to the penthouse and tells my mother, "Moon wants to talk to you, Mama."

"For what?" Mama yelled. "He just needs to send my daughter out here so we can go."

"Nah," Felicia shook her head sadly. "I think you need to talk to him, Ma."

"A'ight, then," Mama kept the gun pointed at Dice and Big Run as she backed into the penthouse.

"Follow me, Ma," Felicia started to walk to the rear of the apartment and my mother followed as instructed.

When they arrived at the last bedroom, Felicia opened the door slowly, and she and my mother walked in. Tracy was lying in the bed asleep. Moon was on one side of the bed and a nurse was on the other. Moon looked up at my mother and then looked back down at Tracy.

"What's wrong with my baby?"

"You tell me, Ms. Simms," Moon said angrily. "Why didn't somebody tell me there was something wrong with her heart?"

"What happened?" Mama asked nervously.

"We was sittin' up here drinkin' and laughin' and then all of a sudden she grabbed her chest and she couldn't breathe."

"Oh my, Lord," Mama started to cry and then turned to the nurse. "Is she going to be OK?"

"Hi, I'm Dr. Campbell. I am Mr. Moon's physician. Tracy is stabilized at the moment, but she needs immediate care. She needs to be in the hospital. Her condition is very, very, serious and if this girl is not treated soon, I'm afraid she may not make it. I'm sorry."

"I'll call an ambulance right now," Mama said.

"Naw, this Cabrini-Green, ain't no ambulance comin' out here. I'll take her."

"OK. But please be careful, Mr. Moon," Dr. Campbell replied. "Any sudden movement could trigger a reaction from her heart."

"I got her." Moon spoke confidently. "I ain't gon' let nothin' happen to her."

"Great. We need to move now."

Moon had an EMT come to the penthouse to get Tracy and transport her to the hospital. People always ask why those in the ghetto commit crimes. The answer is simple. Money and survival. If Moon had not had his drug money, there is no way his doctor would have come to Cabrini-Green to check on a patient. There is also no way an EMT would have come to pick up my sister to transport her to the hospital within an hour, that is, assuming that they would come at all. In Cabrini-Green, medical assistance was not guaranteed. The only guaranteed visits we knew of were trips to the morgue and to the local funeral homes.

Moon always moved in the shadows or stayed low key, so my mother and Felicia rode in the ambulance with Tracy while Moon was inconspicuously chauffeured by Dice and Big Run. When Moon arrived at the hospital, they had already rushed Tracy into surgery. Felicia and my mother were sitting next to each other holding hands. Big Run and Dice remained in the car.

"What they say?" Moon asked.

"They said she need a heart transplant," Mama paused and started to cry once again, as she was realizing the words that were coming out of her mouth. "I ain't got no money for no heart transplant."

"If she needs a heart, we'll get her a heart."

"I know you think you can do anything, son. But not even you can just go around finding hearts. You ain't God."

"Who said I ain't?" Moon looked at Felicia who frowned and shook her head. "Can I see her?"

"She's still in surgery?"

"Then how do you know she needs a heart?"

"I just do."

"Y'all knew it was something wrong with Tracy, didn't y'all?"

"I ain't answerin' none of your questions. What I want to know is, what happened to my baby?"

"What you mean?"

"What happened to her in that apartment?"

"Nothin' happened. My question to you Ms. Simms is, why you lettin' your daughter walk around here like it ain't nothin' wrong with her? Do you know what could happen to her hanging around me and my lifestyle?" Moon whispered sternly and directly. "I don't need that type of trouble around me."

"You don't care nothin' about my daughter. You only thinkin' about yourself. And for the record, I didn't want my daughter hanging around you in the first place."

"You shoulda told her that."

"We did," Felicia snapped.

"Shut up," Moon snapped back. "There's something wrong with Tracy's heart. I need one of y'all to tell me what's wrong."

Felicia and Mama looked at one another and then looked back at Moon. Neither one of them spoke a word.

"Look, you stubborn ass women. I don't give a shit what you think about me, but I don't want anything to happen to Tracy. So I need y'all to tell me what's wrong, so that I can fix it. I ain't gon' be standin' around talkin' to no doctors about this shit."

"We don't need yo' help."

"You know what? Have it your way. But I promise you, you gon' either let me pay for her hospital bills now or her funeral bills later. Just know, if somethin' happens to Tracy, it's on yo' head, Ms. Simms."

Moon shrugged his shoulders and then walked away. As he was exiting, the surgeon entered the ICU to give Felicia and Mama the update on Tracy's condition.

"Ms. Simms?" the surgeon asked.

"Yes, I'm Ms. Simms," Mama said.

"Tracy is stable right now. We uh, we found a condition known as atrial septal defect. It is a hole in the wall between the two upper chambers of your heart. She has probably had this condition since her birth. In some cases, that small atrial defect may close on its own during infancy or early childhood. Unfortunately, that did not happen with Tracy.

"Have you all noticed any recent symptoms where Tracy may have had a shortness of breath, fatigue, swelling of her legs, feet or abdomen? Any heart palpitations or skipped beats?"

"I haven't," Mama answered and then turned to Felicia, "Have you?"

"No, ma'am."

"As it stands, Tracy is going to need a lot of immediate care and she's going to need a transplant...ASAP."

"I know."

"So, you are aware of her condition?"

"Yes."

"Ma'am, I seriously advise you to act immediately. Your insurance should cover most, or at least some, of her medical costs. We can deal with that later. What we need to do now is focus on getting Tracy on that transplant list as quickly as possible."

"I will, doctor."

"We'll get you taken care of at the desk and once we move Tracy to her room, you all can see her and be there for her when she wakes up."

"Thank you," Mama was sad and scared. Felicia was used to seeing her scared, but she was not used to seeing her afraid.

"It'll be OK, Ma," Felicia tried to console my mother.

"Lord, help me."

"We'll get through this somehow, Ma."

"How? I ain't got no insurance. How can we get through this, Felicia?"

"Like we always do...faith."

While my mother and Felicia were consoling one another at the hospital, Stacy and I were sitting in our apartment thinking something had happened to them. As far as we knew, they went to Moon's penthouse to save Tracy and had not returned. We contemplated calling the police, but we knew that was a waste of time. They did not return until daylight the next morning and when they did, Tracy was not with them.

My mother explained to Stacy and me what had happened to Tracy and we were relieved. Tracy had experienced episodes with her heart before and she always bounced back to normalcy. We knew about the heart transplant, but the urgency to have the surgery became much more apparent. Felicia, Stacy and I constantly badgered my mother to accept Moon's help. He was a businessman. Moon knew the business he was in was dangerous and it was important to have two major allies on the payroll, the law and the healers. He had both the money and the influence to get Tracy moved up on that waiting list and to pay for her surgery. But nothing we said convinced my mother to allow Moon the opportunity to save Tracy's life. She thought it was blood money and she wanted no part of it. Little did she know that blood would soon be on her own hands.

After a couple of months of Tracy lying in that hospital bed and those bills piling up, I realized we needed money, so I was going to get it whether my mother liked it or not. I took it upon myself to do something about it. I had turned twelve years old when I went to Moon and told him that I wanted to officially join his gang. He explained to me that once I get in, there is no getting out. He told me that his gang was made of blood brothers. It was blood in, and blood out. In order for me to join, I had to shed someone's blood. If I was to ever leave, it would be my blood that was going to be shed.

My initiation was to settle a dispute between Moon and a former gang member named Dog, who was disrespecting Moon by spreading rumors and questioning his leadership. I was given a gun and a location to find Dog. I was told that he was at a mom-and-pop after hours food joint. Dice drove me to the spot and we sat in the car as I waited for Dog to come out. I was so nervous, my hand would not stop shaking. I wanted to go home and run into my mother's arms and tell her to save me. But then I thought of myself as the man of the house, and when you are the man of the house, sometimes you just have to do what you have to do to survive. In order for my sister to live, Dog was going to have to die.

Dog had a bag of food in his hand heading towards the door. He had his head turned backwards talking to someone, not paying attention to who was watching him. Dice felt that it was perfect timing. I could catch Dog off guard and then run away before anybody had an opportunity to react.

"You ready, lil' nigga?" Dice asked.

"Yeah," I replied nervously.

"Money time. Pull that mask over your face and go handle your business."

I pulled my mask down. I could hear my breathing pounding through my ears. My heartbeat started to reverberate through my chest and into the mask. My head rang from the stress of excitement and fear. Dice pulled up to the curb and waited for me to get out. Dog was standing in the doorway, still laughing and talking with someone inside the café.

"Get out the car, lil' nigga, we ain't got all night."

I took a deep breath and then exited the car. I knew it was all or nothing at that point, so I did not spend any more time thinking. It was time to react and take care of business. I stood in front of the door, only a few feet from Dog. I snatched the door open and without thinking another thought, I fired over and over. I purposely aimed for Dog's legs, because I just did not want to kill a man who had done nothing to me or my family.

Dog fell to the ground and screamed in pain. People scattered, and I ran and jumped into the car with Dice. Dice sped off, and we went riding through the city before heading to Wisconsin so that I could lay low for a while. I wanted to call my mother and let her know I was OK, but they would not let me. Even though Dog did not die, I received word from Moon that he was proud of me for being a standup kid.

I was gone for two days. My mother and sister looked for me but had no idea where to find me. They went to Moon, but he told them that he did not know. When I returned home, I was expecting a whipping or some form of severe punishment, but my mother only asked if I was OK. I told her that I was fine and she left it at that. I knew then that my mother was starting to implode from the pressure. My mother was stressing so badly over Tracy that she was losing grip of herself. She had started drinking heavily to try to cope. But like always in the ghetto, it would always get worse before it ever got better.

Not too long after that, I had pretty much dropped out of school to put those hours in for Moon. By then, I was actually handling product and money because Moon trusted me not to be fool enough to steal his money. One afternoon when I was in the middle of a deal, I heard an agonizing scream come from our apartment. I told my customer that I had an emergency and to wait while I went up to my apartment to check on my family.

When I walked in, Felicia and Stacy were hugging my mother, who had collapsed on the floor. All of them were crying hysterically. I think I already knew what they were about to tell me, but my mind was telling me to delay the inevitable for as long as I could. I slowly stepped toward them, beginning to cry myself.

"What's wrong y'all?" I asked.

"Come 'mere," Felicia opened her arms. "Come 'mere."

I walked over to Felicia, and she took me by the hand and pulled me to the floor with them. I tried to hold on to my last bit of composure before they told me the news. "What's up?"

"Tracy died this afternoon."

"OK," I said.

"Are you OK?" Felicia asked.

"Yeah," I said. I was in complete and utter shock.

"No, you not. Let's go for a walk," Stacy said. Stacy was closer to my age than my other siblings and although we all loved each other equally, we had different relationships. Felicia was like my mother. Tracy was like my big brother. And Stacy was my best friend. "We'll be back, y'all."

"Where y'all going?"

"Nowhere," Stacy smiled. "We'll be back in a little while."

Stacy took me to the candy truck and bought me some ice cream. We ate ice cream and then we walked to the park and she pushed me on the swing. I was allowed to be a kid again, if only for that day.

People from all over the projects came to our apartment and offered their condolences. Our door was opening and closing all day long, and late into the night. The one pressure my mother would not have to worry about for a while was food. We ran out of places to put all the food we received, so we started to give some of it away. After everyone had left and we had carefully secured all of the food and flowers, reality started to settle in...Tracy had died, and she was never coming home.

I laid in my bed unable to go to sleep. The noise from outside never seemed so loud as it did that night. I could hear people talking as if they were in the apartment with me. That noise, the traffic, the life of the projects was usually comforting to me and put me to sleep because it was familiar. It was home. That night everything seemed foreign. In the middle of the night my door opened. Stacy walked in and climbed in the bed with me. She held me and I cried, and I cried and I cried.

As he predicted, Moon ended up paying for Tracy's funeral. As ruthless and diabolical as he was, he lived by a code. Tracy was special to him and he made sure she was buried in a dignified manner. After the funeral, our lives changed forever. Felicia moved out of the projects for the first time in her life. Stacy became the woman of the house. I went back to school and Mama became a chronic alcoholic.

—

"How did the death of your sister affect you?" Dr. Turner asked.

"I was numb. You know, it felt surreal." I said as I contemplated back on that period of my life. "All of these years and it still kind of feels surreal. We were a very closely knitted family."

"You mentioned your mother. She was your hero. How did you feel seeing her go from that strong mother figure to being vulnerable and susceptible to the pressures of your living conditions?"

"I was devastated. Completely devastated. At twelve years old, I felt that I had to fend for myself and take care of my mother. I would see my mother come in some mornings from staying out all night drinking. Only God knows what she was doing and who she was doing it to, but Stacy and I had to take care of each other and take care of my mother. She was sick. Really, really sick. And no matter how much help we tried to get her she wasn't ready to be healed. Sure, she had some days when she was my old mom, but those days were rare."

"How did Felicia fit into your family dynamic after she moved away?"

"She helped us on the bills, and she stopped in from time to time to take care of Mama. She was the only one who could handle her."

"Today was good," Dr. Turner said as she nodded with a smile. "Very good. What do you think?"

"I agree."

"Well, we'll pick up from here next session, OK?"

"OK, looking forward to our next session."

CHAPTER THREE

The summer of 2011...

What "Hey, hey, Dr. Turner, how are you doing?"

"I'm well, how are you today?"

"I'm fantastic. Couldn't be better."

"That's great, you seem to be in a particularly good mood today."

"I am. I am."

"May I ask why?"

"Of course, of course. I had breakfast with all of my siblings for the first time since I left Chicago."

"Wow, that is very good news."

"Yes, we had a ball."

"That being said, let's start from there. Let's go back to your time in Chicago."

"OK...," I said.

—

Seven years after the death of my sister Tracy, my brother Chris was released from prison. At the time of his arrest, he was second in command for all of Chicago for the Gangster Disciples. He had done ten years at Joliet and Statesville on a fifteen-year bid for a manslaughter conviction. He was my idol. My hero. The day he came home was a celebration across the city because his stance against the CPD had become legendary. All of the old heads were hyped to see him. They were expecting him to come out and handle Moon. There were a lot of soldiers who did not like the way Moon was doing business and they wanted him out. My family and I were ecstatic to have Chris back at home with us, but we did not know he had been released until that day he knocked on our door.

"Would one of y'all get that door?" Mama yelled from her bedroom.

Stacy and I still lived at home with my mother, but Felicia had graduated from college and lived in her own place. It was by a happy coincidence that she happened to be there that evening.

"Get the door, boy," Felicia snapped.

"Look, I'mma grown man, stop tryin' to order me around."

"You better get your grown ass over there and open that door. It ain't nobody but one of your little friends."

"Y'all so lazy, I'll get it," Stacy said as she walked to the door. "Who is it?"

"Who you think it is?" Christopher replied.

"Somebody tryin' to be funny. I bet I don't open this door."

"Probably one of Dre's little knucklehead friends playin' around," Felicia chuckled.

"Open the do'!"

"You get the door, Dre, they sound mad."

"Move, girl," I slightly pushed Stacy aside to take my position as the man of the house. I cleared my throat and then said loudly and aggressively, "Who is it?"

"If you don't open up this do', little nigga," Christopher yelled and then chuckled.

My mother slowly walked out of her bedroom and stared at the door and cried, "My baby is home."

"Huh?" I was confused. I thought my mother was delusional from inebriation. But despite her drunken state, she quickly sobered up when she heard my brother's voice.

My mother pushed me out of the way and started unlocking the numerous bolts we had on our door.

"What you doin', Mama?" Felicia asked.

"He's home," Mama said peacefully.

My mother unlocked the final latch and quickly opened the door. Christopher was standing in the doorway with arms open wide and a smile on his face.

"Y'all don't want me to come in or what?" Christopher laughed and we rushed him.

It was pandemonium. The four of us pulled Christopher inside and continued to hug and kiss.

"Whoooooooooa," Christopher laughed out loud, "Y'all tryin' to kill me, man. Get up off me. I ain't talkin' about you, Mama."

Christopher picked my mother up in a bear hug and twirled her around.

"Put me down ol' crazy boy before you drop me."

Christopher lowered my mother to the floor and yelled loudly, "I'M FREEEEE!"

"When you get out, Chris?" Felicia asked.

"Yesterday," Christopher replied.

"Why you wait until today to come over then, boy?" Felicia followed.

"Look, I had some business to handle, Felicia."

"Business? What business is more important than your mama?" Mama joked.

"You know I wasn't talkin' about you, Mama," Christopher smothered my mother with kisses all over her face.

"Stop kissin' on me, boy," Mama said, knowing she could not get enough of Christopher's kisses.

"Look at you, babygirl," Christopher said as he held his arms out to Felicia. Felicia ran into his arms as they embraced and slowly rocked side to side. "You been holdin' it down?"

Felicia pulled away from Christopher and looked him in the face and nodded, "Yeah."

"Look, I'm home now. I'm gon' make sure you finish school and get your degree. Our family need that. You feel me?"

"Yeah," Felicia said as she wiped her eyes. "Thank you, brother."

"It's my job," Christopher looked at me and smiled.

I stood back and watched my brother, my idol, my hero back in the glory of our family's love for him. Like usual, Stacy was in the background with me in our normal chronological pecking order, waiting for her chance to get Christopher's attention.

"'Sup, little nigga?"

Instead of taking my turn to hug my big brother, I gently pushed Stacy in front of me. I think she truly missed Chris more than all of us. She was the one who wrote to him consistently for all ten years of his imprisonment.

"Hey, Chris," Stacy said softly.

"Oh woooooow," Christopher covered his mouth in disbelief and spoke softly. "Stacy? Come 'mere, baby."

Stacy walked into Christopher's arms and finally, he started to cry. My mother and Felicia patted him and Stacy on their backs to console them.

"It's alright, Chris," Mama rubbed Chris' back. "It's alright."

"My baby, my baby, my baby, my baby," Christopher repeated over and over. Christopher pulled away from Stacy and said, "It was…it was your letters that got me through. I don't know what I did for you to be so loyal to me and write and write and write, I mean, every week without fail. You got me through this. No matter what was going on, on the outside, you held me down with your positive and encouraging letters.

"No disrespect to nobody in here, but sometimes I only got one letter a week. Just one letter. And that was from my baby right here."

Christopher hugged Stacy again. The rest of us knew it was their moment, so we stood around and watched them hug in silence. After a while, Christopher peeked over his shoulder and noticed me. He kissed Stacy on the cheek and then smiled at me.

"Come here, lil' nigga." Christopher gestured for me to come to him. "Now, we ain't gon' have no cryin' moment between us. We men. Men don't do that shit."

"Hey boy, I'm still yo' mama!" Mama playfully punched Christopher in the arm.

"Sorry, Mama," Christopher chuckled. "I been in prison for ten years, give a nigga a break."

"Don't get yo' ass whopped on yo' first day out the joint," Mama chuckled back.

"Second day, Mama." Felicia said sarcastically.

"Whatever," Christopher said to Felicia, and then he turned to me. "Let me holla at you for a second, man."

"Where y'all goin'? We ain't through talkin' to you yet," Mama scorned Christopher.

"We be right back, Mama. I just need to have a little private man-to-man talk with my little brother, that's all."

Christopher opened the door for me to follow him outside. I did not know what he wanted to discuss specifically, but I would have blindly followed my brother into hell if that is where he was leading me.

"What's up, man?" I asked.

"Look, what's goin' out here in the hood?"

"What you mean?"

"Who's up now? Who's on top? I lost my channels after these new niggas took over the block. So, what's up?"

"Moon still runnin' it?"

"Moon?"

"Yeah, this been his hood ever since you left."

"What Big Run and Dice doin'? I left this shit in their hands."

"They work for Moon, too."

"How the hell they work for Moon? Moon wasn't nothin' but a snotty nose little kid when I went down."

"He took this street game to a new level, big bruh. He made it a business. Like a company these white dudes be runnin', except he is ruthless. I mean, this nigga will kill yo' mama, yo' daddy, yo' kids, yo' grandmama. Anybody that get in the way of his business will die. It's as simple as that. That nigga is a straight up killa'."

"Moon?" Christopher chuckled.

"Yeah, man…Moon."

"Where do Big Run and Dice hangout?"

"They are Moon's top lieutenants. Big Run is like the businessman and Dice is the hitman."

"I gotta holla at them and check them niggas, man."

"Yoooo', big brother. It ain't like that no more. You can't just go meet with those dudes like that. They have soldiers that you have to send word through to set up a meeting with Big Run and Dice."

"Nigga, I ain't goin' through no peons to talk to those niggas. I raised them in the street life. Where they at?"

"Chris," I said sternly. "You can't come out here like that, man. The streets done changed since you were out here. You will get

smoked in a heartbeat, bruh. Ain't no rules. Ain't no loyalty. The only thing these niggas loyal to now is m-o-n-e-y. Money. That's it. These dudes' body counts are ridiculous."

I respected my brother's street cred and street life, but he was dealing with a different type of animal that he had never encountered before. There had been many Original Gangsters, or OGs, who had come out of prison expecting the same street clout they had when they went in. They tried to step to Moon and his gang and ended up getting smoked. I was trying to get my brother to understand the danger he was facing, but it wasn't registering with him.

"These clowns don't know nothin' about runnin' the streets," Christopher said. "This still my hood and these still my streets. Niggas beware. I'm back and I'm 'bout to take my shit back. You feel me? Now where my other baby sister at?"

Without waiting for a response, Christopher rushed back in the house to inquire about Tracy. In our jubilation at seeing Christopher, we didn't have time to contemplate ways to soften the blow of Tracy's death. Christopher burst through the door, still running on the adrenaline of being a free man, and excitedly asked of Tracy's whereabouts.

"Yo', where my baby, Tracy?"

We looked at each other, waiting for one of us to have the courage to tell Christopher that Tracy had passed.

"What's up? Why y'all lookin' all crazy?" Christopher looked at us with concern. "Where Tracy at?"

"She uh…," Mama tried to find the words, but she could not. She sat down and cried.

Felicia attempted, but just like my mother, she could not bring herself to tell him. I was not even going to try. But the quiet one, the one most likely to remain silent, stepped up because she loved her sister and she loved her brother and she wanted to break the devastating news to him in a loving and caring way.

"Tracy is gone to heaven, Chris," Stacy said softly.

"What you mean, 'gone to heaven', Stacy?"

"Tracy died."

"What happened to her?" Christopher looked at each of us for answers. "How did she die?"

Once again, only Stacy had the ability to answer his questions. "Her heart gave out on her."

"Why didn't nobody tell me?" Christopher looked at my mother.

"I couldn't," Mama said, "you were having a hard-enough time as it was. I just didn't see where telling you would have helped."

"Man, come on, man. Dam." Christopher slumped in a chair and we surrounded him as we cried together.

—

Christopher tried his best to adjust to being on the outside. He stayed inside of our apartment and away from the streets. He went to church. He looked for jobs. His presence seemed to be the remedy for my mother's drinking addiction. She seemed to indulge herself through him. The rest of us never felt a moment of envy due to the fact that our mother's attention was primarily going to only one of her four children. She was sober. Christopher was home, and every single one of us was happy to have a normal family.

It is said that you cannot take a wild animal out of its natural habitat and expect for it to adapt to its new environment. Eventually, it will revert back to what it knows. I am not calling my brother a wild animal, but he was certainly not adaptable to living a crime-free life. When he could not find a job, or a legitimate source of income to provide for him and his family, his criminal instincts took over and he did what he knew best.

By his physical attributes alone, Christopher was an intimidating specimen; he was six-feet, three-inches of solid muscle and he used every inch of his frame to his advantage. Whether it was by force or by choice, Christopher got what Christopher wanted, especially when he felt that it belonged to him.

"Have you seen Big Run or Dice?" Christopher asked.

"Naw, have you?" I replied.

"Naw, I know they know I'm out. For them fools to be runnin' this hood, they sho' hidin' from me."

"Why they hidin' from you? I thought they was your boys?"

"They used to be, but we got some unfinished business."

"Like what?"

"Look, what I'm about to tell you gotta' stay between me and you, you feel me?"

"Cool, what's up?"

"Check it," Christopher prepared to tell me something deep. "Before I went down, I gave Big Run and Dice two-hundid-and-fifty thousand dollars to flip…"

I was so shocked by the amount of money that Christopher had said so casually that I had to interrupt him.

"You had two-hundred and fifty thousand dollars?" I asked excitedly.

"Yeah, calm down, nigga," Christopher chuckled, "two-hundid-and-fifty g's wasn't shit for me. I was movin' shit out like nothin'. I mean, I was that dude, man."

"For   real?"

"Straight up."

"What happened to the money?"

"That's what I need to find out. I gave those dudes two-hundid-fifty grand to flip for me. That night I went down, I told them niggas where my money was and I told them that when I got back, I want my shit. I don't care what they made after my half-a-mil, but I need my money and those niggas are going to pay me my shit or I'm going to end their existence. For real, doe."

"So, what you gon' do?"

"I'mma get my money."

"How? They got a army of soldiers all over Cabrini-Green."

"I don't care who they got. I'mma get my money."

"How, though?"

"I'mma do what I gotta do."

"I don't wanna' sound soft or nothin', but I don't want nothin' to happen to you out here."

"Man, ain't nothin' gon' happen to me. These my streets."

"Whatever you do, I wanna' do it with you."

"Naw, man. This ain't gon' be yo' life."

"It's already my life. I been in these streets since I was ten or eleven years old."

"What you mean?"

"I been workin' for Moon ever since you went down."

I was not expecting Christopher's explosion. It certainly showed a side of him that I had never seen.

"Nigga, what?" Christopher grabbed me and threw me against the wall. "You what?"

"Why…why you so mad?" I struggled to say as Christopher had his huge hands wrapped tightly around my throat. "You…you do it, too."

"You ain't me." Christopher snapped as he pressed his forearm against my throat. "Look, you done with that nigga. You hear me? You done."

"A'ight, man," I mumbled, with Christopher's forearm against my throat.

Christopher removed his arm from my neck and then smoothed my clothes that he had just ruffled.

"Look man, you may not understand what I'm doin' right now, but you will when you get older. This ain't what you think it is out here, little brother. You are getting' outta' here befo' you get caught up." "I'm already caught up. Moon ain't gon' let me out. I belong to him now," I said sorrowfully. "I'm in this for life."

"What you just say to me?"

Before I answered Christopher's question, I wanted to make certain that I worded my point correctly so I wouldn't ignite that fool again.

"What I'm saying is, Moon took me under his wing and looked after me. He told me that it was blood in, and blood out. I was with that. I knew what I was gettin' into. I'm in it for life."

"You killed somebody, man?"

"Blood in, blood out," I repeated.

"Nigga, you crazy? You killin' for this fool while he sittin' up in that ghetto hotel buildin' his life off yo' back?"

"I didn't say I killed nobody."

"Naw, but you keep hollerin' this blood in, blood out shit. Nigga that's over. Startin' today."

"So, you think just because you say somethin' it's gon' happen just like that. Moon ain't gon' let me out. I told you, I ain't got no choice."

"You gotta' choice alright," Christopher looked at me with a grimacing stare. "And I'm tired of talkin' 'bout this shit. You got a choice, lil' nigga', you gon' face me or you gon' face Moon. And if you say me, you better knuckle up right now."

Christopher held his fists in the air and stood in a fighting stance. I was known for being a tough kid, but I was not a fool. My brother would have destroyed me. Moon was a very dangerous man who always followed through on his promises. If he said it was blood in, blood out, he meant it. Nevertheless, if Christopher said I had to face either him or Moon, he meant it. Christopher was standing in front of me, so I decided that I would deal with his threat at that particular time and worry about Moon when I crossed that bridge.

"You tryin' to fight me, bruh?"

"I'm tryin' to save your stupid life."

"By killin' me?" I asked very, very nervously.

"That's your choice. I'd rather you die by my hands, than have the police knockin' on Mama's do' tellin' her to go to the morgue. So, square up, lil' nigga."

"Yo, man, you ain't in prison no mo'. Calm that shit down."

"This my last time square up. 'Cause I'm 'bout to knock yo' ass out."

"Man, I'm not gon' sit up in here and fight my…," the next thing I remember was that I saw the sky and then I saw the ground. I rolled on the ground dazed and confused by the blow my brother had just delivered. The pistol I fell on that I had stuck in the back of my pants did not make my back feel any better either. Had it gone off, I would have most likely died, or at minimum, been paralyzed. "What's wrong with you, man?"

"I don't wanna' hear all that. You gon' deal with me or you gon' deal with Moon?"

"Man, I don't even know what you mean," I said, lying on my back and waiting for him to explain with clarity, before I stood up and he knocked me on my ass again.

"Are you goin' to tell Moon that you out, or do you want me to keep whoopin' yo' ass? It's as simple as that."

"Yeah," I whispered.

"I can't hear you, lil' nigga. What was that?" Christopher yelled.

"I'll tell Moon I'm out."

"Cool," Christopher reached out his hand to help me from the ground.

I was still slightly dizzy when I stood up and stumbled a few steps, before my equilibrium refocused. I repositioned my pistol so that Christopher could not see it. He probably would have taken it and then beaten me with it.

"Dam, Chris, all that wasn't necessary," I said as I rubbed my face.

"Yes, it was. I just saved your life, boy."

"Naw, now Moon's gon' kill me."

"Don't worry about Moon. I'll take care of him."

Speak of the devil and the devil will appear. As my brother was talking, Moon, Big Run and Dice pulled up.

"Yooooooooo'," Big Run yelled from the backseat of the car, "Chris Sims? When you make it back on the block?"

"This nigga know I been back," Christopher whispered to me.

"Let me holla at you, bruh," Big Run followed.

"A'ight," Christopher answered. "You stay here."

"A'ight," I said.

Christopher walked over to the car to talk to Big Run. I was nervous because my brother was like a ticking bomb ready to explode. His old school mentality made him ignorant to the danger of the new school streets. He did not fear Moon or Dice because he felt like he raised them up in the game. Christopher felt like he was legend in our hood. The one thing he did not realize was there was no Hall of Fame for gangsters. There was only jail or cemeteries. If you were not relevant and on top of the game, you may have garnered OG respect, but you would not be a shot-caller. Christopher did not care about being a shot-caller, but he was not going to let anyone else call shots to him.

"Whaddup, dude?" Christopher said as he dapped Big Run.

"My nigga," Big Run said excitedly. "Good to see you, boy."

"Yup, yup," Christopher surveyed the inside of the car as he spoke to Big Run.

"You can't speak, nigga?" Dice, who was sitting in the driver's seat, laughed.

"Whaddup, boy?" Christopher reached through the car behind Moon's head and dapped Dice, accidentally nudging the back of Moon's head. "Move yo' big ass head out the way, lil' nigga."

"Now you know if you were anybody else I woulda' put a hot one in yo' ass, right?" Moon joked. "Whaddup, big bruh?"

When I saw Moon getting out of the car, I thought he was about to deal with my brother right then and there. My heart was pounding. My first reaction was to reach behind me and put my hand on my pistol. If the situation would have escalated, I would have pulled my weapon and started firing at everyone who was not named Christopher. But to my surprise, Moon hugged my brother with sincere and honest respect. Christopher was even surprised.

"You huggin' me or muggin' me, lil' nigga?" Christopher joked to Moon.

"We need to break bread, big bruh. I gotta' tell you some shit on the hood, for real though."

"Fa sho," Christopher said. "I hear you the man out here right now."

"I just do what I do," Moon raised his hands in the air. "But you the man that made the man."

"We need to sit down and talk for real, lil' bruh. No disrespect, but right now, I need to holla at Run for a minute, cool?"

"Fa sho." Moon nodded in agreement. "Your old head niggas need to relive them good ol' school days."

Christopher and Big Run walked away to talk privately. I was still watching from afar. Maybe I had been wrong about my brother. Maybe he was a legend. I had never heard Moon give anyone props. Never. Nor had I ever heard him laugh or joke out loud. Christopher must have left one hell of an impression on Moon for him to show such public respect. Meanwhile, it was time for my brother to deal with Big Run.

"Whaddup, Chris?" Big Run spoke playfully.

"Naw, dog, don't whaddup me. Where my money, nigga?" Christopher snapped.

"Yo, bruh, you need to bring that down a little. Who you talkin' to like that?"

"You, nigga. Where my gotdam money?" Chris walked closer towards Big Run until they stood nose to nose.

"Don't walk up on me, Chris," Big Run stepped back and stood in a fighting position.

"What you gon' do, little punk?" Chris yelled directly into Big Run's face.

"I ain't gon' be too many of your punks, nigga," Big Run shouted back.

"Cool," Chris swung and connected to the side of Big Run's head, sending him to the ground in an unconscious state. People continued on their way by as if nothing had happened.

"Now was all that necessary?" Moon said as he came running, laughing and shaking his head.

"This fool owes me money, lil' bruh. You know how it is. Nothin' personal."

"Not in front of the hood though, Chris. You a fool, boy," Moon laughed again.

"Yo, Dice, come 'mere and let me holla at you," Chris yelled to Dice still sitting in the car.

"Naw, you come to me."

"Cool," Chris starts to walk towards Dice.

"Dice owe you money, too?" Moon asked.

"Yup," Chris replied without looking at Moon, still walking towards Dice.

"Now you know that fool strapped, don't you?" Moon said a little louder.

"Always."

"And you gon' walk up to that nigga anyway?"

"He ain't the only one strapped. And he sittin' in the car."

"Hold on, John Wayne, I don't need these kinda' problems on my block unless they my problems, nigga. Yo, Dice?" Moon yelled.

"Yeah?"

"Come 'mere, dog."

Dice gets out of the car and adjusts the gun hidden in the back of his pants waist. I stood back with my hand on my gun. I did not know what was about to happen, but I was prepared for anything.

"What's up, Moon?" Dice asked.

"Chris said you and Big Run into him for…," Moon looks at Chris, "how much you say they hit you for?"

"Two hundred and Fifty grand."

"What you gotta' say for yourself, Dice?"

"Shit went left. He gave us some loot to flip and the cops bust us before we could re-up and then he did his bid at State," Dice shrugged his shoulders. "Niggas forgot."

"How we gon' fix this 'cause you two niggas'll kill first and ask questions later?" Moon asked Chris and Dice.

"Easy. They give me my money and it's over."

"Dice?" Moon asked.

"I ain't got two hundred and fifty-thousand dollars layin' around like that."

"Tell you what?" Moon put his hand on Chris' shoulder. "Stop by the penthouse tonight and I'll have your money and we can end this shit before it even starts."

"You gon' pay their debt?" Chris asked.

"Think of it more like I'm payin' you back for bringing me up."

"As long as I get my loot, I don't give a damn how we think of it," Chris joked.

"So we ending all of the bullshit, right?"

"Fa sho," Chris smiled and dapped Dice.

"I'm good," Dice answered.

"Now wake that fool up. He's embarrassing me out here," Moon stepped over Big Run's unconscious body and walked back to their car. Dice sat Big Run up and slapped his face a few times until he responded. Chris stood over them with his arms folded.

"What happened?" Big Run asked incoherently.

"Chris knocked yo' ass out," Dice chuckled.

"Man, what you hit me for?" Big Run shouted angrily.

"Nigga, you know how this go," Chris spoke sternly.

"You stole on me though, Chris."

"Ain't nobody steal on you, lil' nigga. You runnin' yo' mouth instead of puttin' in work," Chris and Dice laughed out loud.

"I wasn't even gon' talk to that strong ass nigga, bruh. I was going to pop his ass as soon as he walked up on me," Dice laughed.

"Yeah, see, I was coming at you a little different. I know how you livin' out here. I brought you up out here," Chris said.

"I'mma steal on yo' ass when you least expect it, nigga. Believe that," Big Run said, still sitting on the ground.

"So, you back on the block for real or you goin' straight?" Dice asked.

"I tried to go straight, but they won't let me. I looked for jobs, but they keep giving me this ex-convict bullshit. How they expect for a nigga to go straight when he can't take care of his self?"

"Yo, Moon got love for you, bruh. You ain't gotta' beg nobody for shit out here. Come over here with us." Big Run said as Chris helped him to his feet.

"I can't work for a nigga that use to work for me, nigga."

"It's better than sittin' around beggin' these white fools for a fifty-cent ass job that still can't feed yo' family," Dice said.

"Man, I gotta' family though, bruh."

"Yeah, you gotta' hungry family," Dice insisted.

"Look, I'mma talk to Moon and see what he talkin' 'bout, but it gotta be worth my time. I ain't gon' be out here workin', riskin' my freedom over some smalltime bullshit."

"You know Moon gon' put you on big time, fool. You the only nigga he respects out here."

"Tell him I come through later on."

"Fa sho," Big Run said.

"Yo, man, you know that shit was only business, right, Run?"

"That was family. If it was business, I'd be blastin' yo' ass. You took a case for all of us 'cause we family, and if a nigga let a little lil' slap boxing breaks up family, he a straight bitch."

"I'll see y'all later at the penthouse."

"A'ight, nigga," Dice said.

"Peace, my nigga." Big Run said.

—

Later on, at the penthouse, Moon had a small party where he shipped in strippers to perform for him and his crew. Big Run and Dice were enjoying themselves, as they had plenty of soldiers to protect Moon. Chris was in the background casing the apartment and observing everyone's activities. When some of the strippers approached him for a lap dance, he would decline them and continue to observe everybody and everything that was happening at the party.

Chris and Moon barely spoke to one another throughout the night. They looked, nodded and then smiled. Moon seemed to be seeking approval as a boss leader from Chris. It was a case of two alpha males, both waiting for the other to approach first. Their egos would have probably let the entire night pass without them saying a word to one another, had it not been for one small distraction…me.

I was eighteen and I felt that I was as grown as anyone there. As I was making my rounds, drinking and collecting lap dances, I happened to walk between Moon and Chris simultaneously. Both asked me questions at the same time.

"Yoooo', you snuck outta' the house?" Moon asked.

"What yo' lil' ass doing up in here?" Chris asked.

"Partying like you, nigga," I said.

"Take yo' ass home."

"He's a grown ass man, Chris. Let him hang with the big boys."

"Let me holla at you for a second, Moon." Chris said solemnly.

"Sound serious, let's step in my office."

Chris followed Moon back to his office. Once again, I was stressing out over a potential confrontation between my brother and my boss. Both were fearless and dangerous. All that I could do was stand outside Moon's office and hope everything went well. They had certainly killed my vibe for the party.

"Sound serious out there, big dawg, whaddup?" Moon asked.

"My little brother, Moon. You gotta' let him out."

"Come on, Chris. You know I can't do that. I like the kid personally. He reminds me of me when I was his age. But this is business, man. You know I can't let him out. Only one way out and you know what that way is."

"I'm out."

"Naw, you ain't never out either. You just got respect. From me and the streets."

"Tell you what, Moon, take me."

"Take you where?"

"I'll move into my brother's spot."

"You know you ain't gon' stand on no corner hustling, Chris," Moon laughed. "I wouldn't even let you do that, nigga."

"You right. I won't do that. But I can be that man."

"And what man is that, big dawg?"

"You handle your business and I will handle your streets."

"Hmm, now that's interesting. Now you have my attention. What does uh…what does, 'that man' mean to you?"

"That means I'm responsible for everything that happens on the streets. If any bodies have to be took, I'm takin' 'em. Any cases have to be took, I'm takin' em. All of these knuckleheads you got out there now ain't shit man, you know that."

"Look like we may be able to do business, big dawg."

"What about Big Run and Dice? They think they co-second in command. How we gon' handle them?"

"I ain't handlin' shit. You handle the streets, remember? You handle them fools."

"That ain't nothin' but somethin' to do. Consider it done."

"Big Run ain't about shit. I keep him on 'cause he real family. But that nigga, Dice, he trigger happy. He'll put a hot one in just for the hell of it."

"I ain't trying to hear that shit, man. I eat niggas like that for breakfast."

"Yeah, boy, I heard about your body count. That shit is insane," Moon laughed.

"Strictly business. Well, some of that shit was strictly personal," Chris laughed.

"Yo, back to lil' man. If we do this, you gotta' get him out of town, like ASAP, you feel me? We may be cool with this, but I can't have the streets questioning me."

"Where he gon' go, bruh?"

"I don't know. Send that lil' nigga to the Army, the Air Force, or some shit. He needs the discipline anyway."

"I know you bull shititn', but that's where he needs to be."

"Actually, I wasn't. I believe that's where he belongs. Let's go set that joker straight. Tell his hustlin' ass he about to be up outta' here," Moon joked.

"Followin' you, sir."

Chris and Moon made a beeline straight to me. They called me back to the office and told me my future. I was mad as hell. I did not want to be in anybody's army. I wanted to come up in the streets like my big brother. I was highly pissed off.

Chris took me to the Marine Corps recruiting station, and I took a physical and a test, and passed both. They gave me two weeks to make up my mind, or I would be a United States Marine. I tried everything I could to stay home. I went to Felicia and Stacy to try to get them on my side, but neither one bought in. They felt that getting out of Cabrini-Green was not good enough. I needed to get out of Chicago and out of the state of Illinois. I went to my mother to save me, but she was on one of her drinking binges and was totally incoherent.

She was laid out on the kitchen floor. I shook her to try to get her to stand, so that I could help her to her bedroom. When I rolled her over, I saw that vomit had almost covered her body completely from her neck to her feet. I knew instantly that this was not a normal drunken episode. I started to shake my mother more rigidly. I sat her up and started to slap her face, but she was still unresponsive.

I panicked and did not know what to do, so I ran downstairs and told Chris. Chris and I ran upstairs. He tried to revive my mother as well, but to no avail. Chris told me to grab my mother's ankles while he picked her up by her shoulders. Once we were off of the elevator, Chris picked her up and we ran to the car where Dice and Big Run were sitting.

"Yo, get me to the hospital, now," Chris screamed.

"What's wrong with yo' mama, man?" Big Run asked.

"I don't know, just go. GO! GO! GO!"

Dice kicked the car in gear, and we sped away. When we arrived at the hospital, I called Felicia and told her about my mother. Felicia picked up Stacy on her way and they met us at the hospital. My mother was placed on a ventilator. Eventually, we asked that the ventilator be removed so that her life could take its natural course. The four of us surrounded her at her bedside. She temporarily regained consciousness, looked at us and reached out her hands. We held her hands and she blinked her eyes a few times as if she were trying to fight death, and then she closed her eyes for the final time.

My mother's death seemed to zap all of the street out of me. Without her, I no longer wanted to be in Cabrini-Green. I no longer wanted the street life. I wanted completely out. I wanted to go as far away as possible. My ticket out was the Marines and I took it. We buried my mother on a Friday afternoon, and I spent Friday night with my sisters and brothers. At daybreak on the following Saturday morning, I was on a plane heading to Parris Island, South Carolina.

—

"How did the death of your mother affect you?" Dr. Turner asked.

"I thought after Tracy's death, I would be prepared for the next family member to die, especially my mother. We knew what path she was on. But like the old adage says, you can try to prepare for death all that you want. But there is no preparation for a loved one's death because it is that absence which has no substitute. I just needed to get away. Far, far, away. And the Marines was exactly what I needed."

"How was your transition to the military?"

"Culture shock."

"I see," Dr. Turner said, as she nodded with a smile. "I definitely want to know how you were able to transition from the streets of Cabrini-Green to the discipline of the military. Well, we'll pick up from here next session, OK?"

"OK."

"Great."

CHAPTER FOUR

The summer of 2011...

W hat "Good afternoon, Mr. Simms. How are you?"

"Good afternoon, Dr. Turner," I said in a melancholy tone. I was not in the best of moods that day and I had to force myself to attend our session.

"I'm fantastic," I tried to smile, but failed miserably. "Couldn't be better."

Dr. Turner noticed my mood immediately, "Is everything OK, Mr. Simms?"

"I'm fine."

"OK," Dr. Turner paused momentarily and then continued, "At our last session, you were telling me about your transition from the streets of Chicago, to the strict discipline of the military?"

"Oh, yeah."

"Care to share?" Dr. Turner asked lightheartedly.

"Well..."

—

I arrived at Parris Island, South Carolina in the fall of 1983. My first night was a complete culture shock. Around four in the morning, the drill instructors ran in our dorm and started yelling and screaming for us to get on our feet. At first, I thought I was dreaming. I mean, it was like a loud, confusing nightmare. I was

used to my mother's loud screaming, but this was on a whole other level. After we were awake, the constant screaming continued. That's when I learned the practice of hurry-up and wait. For the life of me, I could not understand why there was such an extreme sense of urgency to get from one place to another, but then once we arrived, we had to wait on our drill instructors.

I started off on the wrong foot from the very beginning of boot camp. I was lazy and I wanted to do things my way. That did not sit well with my drill instructors. And as much of a point that I had to prove to them that I was a tough kid from the streets of Chicago, they had an even greater point to prove that I was nothing more than another street punk who would do it the Corp way, or find my ass heading back to Chicago or the brig. I would have preferred Chicago, but the Marine Corps had other plans.

I had goofed off during boot camp and so became known as Beetle Bailey, a slouch and slacker military cartoon strip character. I did not care what the other Marines thought of me, because I was trying to make my way back to Chicago anyway. When we were taking our first test, I had planned to sabotage my PT, physical training, so miserably that they would have to send me back home.

"Private Simms? What the hell are you doing?" Sgt. Mason screamed at me for not keeping up with the rest of the squad.

Drill Instructor, aka Sergeant Mason, aka Sarge, was a mountain of a man. He was a huge white guy with a perfect crew cut, who was as mean as an angry tiger. If one of us felt like we were having a bad day and we wanted to try a drill instructor, Sergeant Mason was not the one to try and build your reputation on.

"I'm running as fast as I can, sir."

"Well, you better learn how to run faster if you plan on stayin' in my Marine Corps. Now move your ass…NOW."

"I can't, sir…I can't go no faster, sir."

"Ain't no such word in the Marine vocabulary as can't, Private Simms. Do you understand me?"

"Sir, yes, sir."

"I'mma run yo' ass all the way to the finish line. And you better catch up with the rest of your platoon, 'cause if you embarrass me by putting me in last place, I'mma have your sorry ass wipe up every single grain of sand on every single beach from Florida to Maine, do you understand me, Private Simms?"

"Sir, yes, sir."

Although I wanted to sabotage my test, I was still not prepared for even the start of the two-mile run, let alone to fake an injury or pretend I was winded. I was not used to running for exercise. All the running I did was from the cops, and that was always a short sprint. I was so exhausted that I started to have delusions. I thought I saw my deceased sister and mother standing in front of me urging me to continue. I wanted to give up and go home. The streets gave you very few options, but there was always a way out of trouble if you were willing to do what the streets wanted you to do for redemption. If the streets did not want you anymore because there was no way of resolving your trouble, you do what Chris and Moon made me do…you get the hell out and do not look back. Until that day, I had never been in a position where I truly felt that I had no options and nowhere to run. I felt more from those drill instructors than I did from some of those clowns who pulled guns on me in Chicago.

Sergeant Mason was a hard-ass and he had not given me one single break. It seems like I could not even shit right, without him getting on my ass. That day was no different from any of the others.

"I feel like I'm 'bout to throw up, sir," I mumbled, as my stomach started to bubble.

"You better not throw up on my street, Private Simms. Do you hear me?" Sgt. Mason screamed, while running beside me, with his face only centimeters from mine.

"Yessir," I screamed back.

"You think I'mma let you hurl on my street, Private Simms?"

"Sir, no, sir."

"Huh? I can't hear you Private Simms. Do you think I'm gon' let you hurl all on my pretty streets?"

"Sir, no, sir."

"Well, then I suggest you take your throw up, suck it back up in your mouth, and swallow that shit. Do you understand me, Private Simms?"

"Sir, yes, sir."

"Now mooooooooooooooooooooooove."

As tired as I was, I picked up my feet and I started to run. The faster Sergeant Mason ran, the faster I ran. I did not want to disappoint Sergeant Mason and deep inside. I did not want to be the last Marine to finish his two-mile test. However, when I finally saw the finish line, I realized that I had spent too much time slacking off because there was absolutely no one in sight. I crossed the line and then bent over from exhaustion.

"Sorry, Sarge," I said breathlessly.

"What you sorry for, Private?"

"I tried to catch up, sir." I said between breaths.

"Catch up to who?" Sgt. Mason asked with confusion.

"My platoon, sir."

"Catch up?" Sgt. Mason chuckled. "Well, hell, Marine, here come your platoon right now."

Sergeant Mason pointed in the direction of my platoon as the first of them to complete were turning the corner and coming down the homestretch to the finish line. I looked at Sergeant Mason with confusion and excitement.

"Did I…?" I was so surprised that I could not even express myself.

"Yup. You were the first to finish."

"But how, sir? When?" I asked.

"Let this be a lesson to you, Marine. Never give less than what you have to give. You can only find out how much you have to give by giving it your all. Now for as long as you are in my Marine Corps, you better revere it and respect it. Do you see what you can do when you put your mind to it, son?"

"Sir, yes, sir," I said as the rest of my platoon started to finish their run. "Thank you, sir."

"What the hell you are thanking me for?" Sgt. Mason snapped. "You did this yourself. And I better not see anything less from you for as long as you wear that uniform. Am I making myself clear, Private Simms?"

"Sir, yes, sir," I yelled proudly.

"A'ight, then," Sgt. Mason walked away as if it was just another day.

Perhaps for Sergeant Mason it was, but for me, it was a life-altering experience. The fact that he cared so much about me as an individual to run my entire two miles beside me showed me that someone other than my family cared about me and believed in me. During the rest of my boot camp, I was a standout Marine who became squad leader, then platoon leader. I found out later that Sergeant Mason was a former Chicago Police officer who had been on the Cabrini-Green beat. He was one of the rare and good ones who actually cared about people. He rejoined the Marines after he realized that he and the Chicago Police Department had two different agendas. Sergeant Mason changed my life, and I will forever be indebted to him for caring about a young, black and misguided teenager from the projects.

After I completed boot camp, I could not wait to get back home and show everybody in Cabrini-Green what I had accomplished. When I landed at O'Hare Airport, I was so excited that I wanted to leap out of the plane's window because I was too impatient to wait for everyone aboard the plane to exit. My brother and my two sisters were picking me up, and we were going to go out and eat in style. This was pre-9/11, so they were able to meet me at the gate. When I walked through the gate, Chris, Felicia and Stacy were standing side-by-side. They were dressed like they were on their way to church. I ran to them and they hugged me. It was good to be home, but it was even better to be around my family.

"Look at you, boy," Christopher twirled me around. "The Marines done put some weight on you."

"My little brother is a grown man," Felicia added.

"We can't call you little brother anymore," Stacy said. "You're bigger than Chris now."

"Yeah," Christopher pushed me playfully, "but don't try me, lil' nigga', mess around and get that ass smoked. I'm too old to try to wrestle yo' big ass."

"I'm hungry. Where the eats?"

"Where you wanna' go?" Felicia asked.

"I don't care. Let's just eat."

We ended up going to a restaurant near downtown Chicago. It was very elegant and clean; upscale to say the least. I had traveled across the country and dined in some of the fanciest restaurants in America, but never in the city of Chicago.

"This is sweeeeeeeet," I said, looking around. "Who picked this restaurant?"

"Who you think?" Stacy said sarcastically.

"Felicia bougie ass," Christopher said.

"Why do I have to be bougie because I like nice things?"

"Because even when yo' ass was in CB, everybody had those free backpacks, but you had to accessorize yours with glitter and sparkles and shit, talkin' 'bout you Diana Ross on 'Mahogany.'"

"Look, don't make me show my CB ass up in this restaurant, boy," Felicia laughed. "You may wanna' leave Cabrini-Green Felicia where she is."

"Dam," I laughed. "I guess she told you, big brother."

"Please keep CB Felicia wherever she is," Stacy added.

"Man, it's good to see y'all," I said, as I looked around the table at each one of my siblings. "I just wish…"

I took a moment to compose myself because I was feeling overwhelmed by the memory of my mother and sister.

"What's the matter, Dre?" Stacy asked.

"I was just, uh," I paused again to compose myself. "I was just thinking about Mama and Tracy and wishing they were here."

"Oh," Stacy replied sadly. "I'm sure they are looking down on you, and they are proud as they can be."

"I practically raised you, so you know I'm proud of you," Felicia kissed me on the cheek.

"I'm proud of your ol' knucklehead ass, too, babyboy," Christopher patted me on the back…hard.

"Why you always gotta' be so ghetto, Chris?" Felicia snapped. "Leave that shit at Cabrini-Green, OK?"

"Oh, so you move to the north side and now you too good for CB?"

"Yup. I was always too good. And so was the rest of you. They piled us on top of each other like caged animals and wanted us to survive off of killing one another. You think I'm supposed to be proud of that shit, Chris? Hell yeah, I'm too good for Cabrini-Green."

"That's your home, Felicia. Cabrini-Green made you who you are. Claim it," Christopher raised his voice.

"I ain't claiming shit. I am not who I am because of Cabrini-Green. I am who I am, in spite of Cabrini-Green. You can claim it all you want, but there's nothing there for me but bad memories and hard times, and I ain't never goin' back there. NEVER!"

"Whoooooa, it ain't that deep, Felicia," I interrupted. "Y'all trippin'."

"No, she trippin'," Christopher yelled.

"Lower your voice, Chris," Stacy whispered.

"Why I gotta' lower my voice? I don't care what these white folks think about me. They don't know me."

"Bruh?" I said. "You a'ight?"

"I just get tired of hearing people talkin' about the hood like people in the hood wanna' be there. Some of us ain't got no choice. You think America care about a nigga wit' a record? Hell naw. So for us niggas that gotta live in the streets, we don't need to be hearing this shit about us. Cabrini-Green ain't just a project. It's people, gotdammit. And people gotta' live. And you talkin' about how bad it is, Felicia, what you doin' to help those people still livin' there? Not shit."

"I ain't killin' 'em like you, that's for dam sho'."

"OK, that's it," Stacy snapped. Every one of us stopped talking and looked at Stacy, because we were not used to her being aggressive. "We are not here for this stupid family drama. We are here to celebrate our little brother's return home. So please stop being so selfish by dominating his homecoming with your own personal drama. OK?"

"You need to talk to your big brother, Stacy," Felicia mumbled.

"Really, Felicia?" Stacy asked in disbelief. "Both of you need to apologize."

"UGHHH," Felicia snarled. "Sorry, Dre."

"Yo, sorry, babyboy," Christopher said.

"Let's just eat and have fun, OK?" I tried to piggyback off of Stacy and just bring the moment back to family. "The only thing that matters is that I'm home and we're all together hangin' out."

"Right," Stacy added.

"So, my little brother is a United States Marine?" Christopher asked.

"Yup. Ooh-Rah," I yelled.

"I have a question, everybody," Stacy said.

"What's up?" Felicia asked.

"Can we please eat? I am hun-guh-ree."

"That's what I'm saying," I chuckled and grabbed my silverware. "Eat up."

After dinner, Christopher and I went driving through Cabrini-Green. My sisters had warned me not to go, but it was as much a part of me as my DNA. I could not resist the urge to return to my old stomping grounds and see my neighborhood. As much as Felicia and Stacy hated it, Christopher and I needed it.

"So, what's going on out here, big bruh?"

"A lot of shit has changed in six months, babyboy."

"Like what?"

"Dice went loco on us and I gotta' put him down."

"Where is he?"

"He out there somewhere. I'mma find him. He can't hide."

"What he do?"

"What he do? You ain't heard?"

"How the hell I'mma know street shit when I'm away in the Marines, Chris?" I joked.

"Yo, man, shit got real out here, man. When Moon promoted me to second in command, Big Run was cool wit' it. That nigga didn't want to deal with the pressure anyway. But Dice, man, that fool went wild out here. He just started killin' niggas for no reason."

"I ain't never trust that nigga anyway. So, what you gon' do?"

"End that nigga career. He gotta' go."

"Straight like that?" I asked.

"Yup. Straight like that."

"What's up with Moon?"

"He straight. He wanna see you while you here."

"For real?"

"Yeah. I've seen that brotha' do some inhumane shit to people. Straight up, heartless assassin. But for some reason, that nigga love you."

"For real?"

"Straight up," Christopher nodded as he turned into the Cabrini-Green projects. "That's why I respect him."

"I woulda' never thought you could work for Moon. I thought one of y'all woulda' killed each other by now."

"As long as a nigga respect me, I can respect him. Moon understand what I bring to the table. I'm loyal. I'm fearless.

And

I'm about my business. Shit, I know more about the game than him. But Moon got that book sense and he got common sense. All I know is the streets. Moon know the boardroom, too. He can make shit happen that I can't. So if I can get broke off by being second in command behind a loyal nigga and not have to fight for every crumb I get, I'mma make that business move. You feel me?"

"Yeah, that's smart."

As we pull up to Moon's building, there were a lot of men standing guard outside. There was no way anyone was going to get close to Moon without having to go to war with his street army, not even the police. I was impressed for all of the wrong reasons.

Christopher and I took the elevator to Moon's penthouse where there was more security. I was proud to see all of the soldiers dapping Christopher and showing him respect. He had become who I wanted to be. I knew a lot of the old soldiers, but Christopher introduced me to some of the new soldiers as well. Due to my excitement by the attention Christopher was receiving, I fantasized about returning home and taking over Moon's rule when he decided to step down.

When we entered Moon's penthouse, it was like entering the Playboy Mansion. There were naked women, alcohol and drugs everywhere. I was slightly intimidated, but I was not going to let Christopher know. I grabbed a bottle of something, I do not even know what it was, and turned it up. Christopher put his arms around my shoulders and led me to the back of the penthouse where Moon was sitting with two naked women.

"Babyboy?" Moon shouted. "What's up wit' you, lil' nigga?"

"Hey, Moon, what's up?" I was surprised when Moon hugged me.

"You done got all swole on me, boy," Moon squeezed my arms.

"He tried to try me, Moon," Christopher joked.

"I believe you can beat his ass, babyboy," Moon joked.

"Don't get that boy ass whooped up in here, Moon," Christopher joked back.

"I get paid to fight for America. I ain't got time to be fighting you common ass niggas."

"Ohhhh, it's like that? You hear this cocky lil' nigga, Chris? Sound just like yo' ass."

"Gotdam right."

"Hey, let's ride out for a minute. This shit is depressin'," Moon said.

Moon, Chris and I went for a ride with massive security in front of us and behind us. It was never like that when I worked for him. I asked myself how Moon could blow up so big in such a short time? But after seeing the chemistry between Moon and Chris, I understood. You have two alpha male personalities who are smart enough to realize that without the help of the other, they both could not be as successful as their potential allowed. Since it was Moon's business, Christopher accepted his role and they prospered.

"When we retire this will all belong to you, Babyboy," Moon said.

"Right," Christopher agreed.

"Cool...cool."

"But you have to do it a different way," Moon said.

"What you mean?" I asked.

"The streets is always gon' be the streets. You can't legitimize that shit. But an individual can legitimize himself. That's what you gon' do. You gon' take our street shit and make it legitimate."

"How?" I asked.

"Don't worry about how," Chris chuckled. "Just know that we ain't in this shit just to be gangsta' niggas. We got a goal. All that shit Felicia was talkin'? It was straight bullshit. If CB hadn't showed me what to do, I wouldn't know shit. But right now, in just six months, I make more than Felicia will make in ten years. You make your money and you get the hell out."

"But I thought y'all said it was only one out?"

"It is for a dumb nigga," Moon answered.

We pulled up to a traffic light that was just turning red. We were the second vehicle in a caravan of three. We paid no attention to the cars pulling beside us. A big van pulled up to our passenger side and stopped. That was the only side where the enter and exit door was located. As Moon was talking, I noticed the van's door start to open. I found it strange for the door to be opening during a traffic light stop. From that moment everything seemed to happen in slow motion. Moon was sitting on the left driver's side near the window. I was sitting in the middle and Christopher was sitting on the passenger side next to the door.

"Fellas?" I said nervously. "I think y'all need to…"

Before I could complete my sentence, the door flung open and there was a man wearing a black mask holding a high-powered weapon in his hands. He opened fire on us and sprayed our vehicle with bullets. Instinctively, Christopher jumped on top of Moon and I to shield us from the gunfire. I was trying to push him off of me to remove him from harm's way, but he wouldn't release his grip on the front of the backseat and the back of the front seat. The firing stopped and the shooter removed his mask. It was Dice. I looked him directly in the eyes as he smiled at me and then gave me a menacing frown as the van pulled away.

"SHIT! GO! GET TO HOSPITAL! NOW! GO! GO! GO!" Moon screamed.

The car pulled away from the traffic and zoomed towards the hospital. I held Christopher's bullet-riddled body in my arms.

"You are alright?" Christopher asked as he coughed up blood.

"I'm fine. I'm good," I cried, "You gon' be alright, too. Just hold on. Just hold on. Alright? Just hold on."

As we were getting closer to the hospital, Moon had to cover his ass to make sure that he did not get implicated in the shooting.

"Look, babyboy, I can't get caught up in this shit. Take yo' brother in this hospital and tell them it was a random shooting. Don't worry about nothin' else. That's all you say. You hear me?"

"Yeah, but I saw who did it. It was Dice."

"You didn't see shit. You take care of Chris. I got this shit. We don't need the cops to take care of street shit. You don't know nothin'. Now, do you hear me?"

"Yeah, but…"

"Ain't no buts. I got this shit," Moon screamed. As the car screeched its way into the Emergency Room parking lot, Moon pulled out his gun and looked at me. "This shit will end tonight. Get out."

Two of Moon's soldiers jumped out of the car and helped me take Chris into the Emergency Room. The attendants rushed to him, and he had immediate surgery. They did their best, but Chris' organs had suffered too many injuries to recover. He died two days later. On the third day, they found Dice's body hanging from a telephone pole. He had been decapitated and mutilated, with his arms and legs also missing.

After Chris' funeral, I went back to the Marines. I was not afraid or nervous on my return. Instead, I was angry. I did not want to learn discipline any longer. I wanted to learn how to kill. There were more people involved in Chris' death than Dice, and I wanted them all to die.

—

In 1984, I arrived at Camp Lejeune for my School of Infantry instruction. Instinctively, I wanted to learn and experience as much combat as possible. My plan was to return to the streets of Chicago with a knowledge of warfare that the projects had never seen. Although I had been redirected, I had not been fully rehabilitated. I wanted to become a deadly weapon, so I signed up for every active form of training for which I could qualify.

In 1988, I went to the jungles of Panama for warfare training. It was hot and steamy my entire time there. This was not an assimilated training where we had access to MRE's (Meals Ready to Eat) and convenient supplies for hygiene and medical care. This was real-life tactical training in real-life combat conditions. I learned to survive in the wild and live off of the land. I envisioned myself as being at war with the police or a rival gang, and I thrived in that environment. I withstood the heat. I withstood the storms. I withstood starvation. I withstood circumstances that I did not even know existed, and I was only nineteen years old. Still, I wanted to learn more.

After several attempts, I finagled my way into Scout Sniper Training. I was based at Camp Fuji, Japan in June of 1990. Due to the nature of the sniper's mission, we must be trained mentally and physically to function independently. I was taught three phases of training. The first involved land navigation and marksmanship. During this phase, trainees fire sniper ammunition on long distance and unknown distance qualification courses. The second phase covers stalking techniques, field skills and calls for fire rehearsals. The third phase encompasses everything from communication to surveillance performance. In September of that same year, during my Scout Sniper Training, I was called to the Iraqi War. I fought in Iraq for a few months, then I was shipped back to Japan to complete my training there.

Upon my return to Japan, a lady friend of mine whom I had been seeing off and on, informed me that she was pregnant. At first, I was stunned. I was shocked. I had questions that I needed answered. Nevertheless, I went forward in the role of father. Several months later, my first child, Khloe, was born. Her mother was in the United States Army. I met her mother in Japan...mainland Japan, which is probably about fifteen minutes away from Tokyo, Japan. Being that she was in the United States Army and I was in the United States Marines, we had the rivalry of service branches, but the familiarity of our home country. Some of my fellow Marines would call me a traitor for mating with an Army G.I. Shit...but once they saw her, trust me, they totally understood.

That was a beautiful experience. I was not there for the birth because I was leaving to go back to the States to go to war. I was leaving to be stationed at Camp Pendleton in California, and I was on my way to war. I did not get a chance to see the birth of my first biological child, my oldest daughter Khloe.

—

"And what questions did you need answered, Mr. Simms?" Dr. Turner asked.

"The first obvious questions were, is she really pregnant and if she was, was the child really mine?"

"Were you able to get those questions answered?"

"Eventually…yes," I paused momentarily and then continued. "But with us being in Japan, there were legal ramifications that complicated our situation."

"Such as?"

"You know, pregnancy confirmation, DNA confirmation, paternal parental rights, financial allotments, it was all thrown at me all at once."

"I understand," Dr. Turner said. "And how were you able to deal with all of that pressure?"

"Well…," I paused momentarily.

"Take your time, Mr. Simms."

"Well, I certainly didn't deal with it as well as I should have. Like I said, my brother was killed. I was sent to the war. I had a lot of serious things going on, but I managed to pull everything together and get them under control."

"And what aboooout?" Dr. Turner said, dragging her words, trying to recall if I had mentioned my child's mother's name.

"Her name is Clarice."

"Clarice is a nice name."

"I'm sure she would appreciate you saying that," I said, sarcastically.

"Let's stop here and pick back up from this very spot next week?"

"Sounds good to me."

"I have an idea," Dr. Turner said as she twirled her foot in circles, "If you would like to explore a new exercise, I think it would be very productive for you and your girls."

"Sure, anything," I responded anxiously.

"Next week, how about you bring Khloe and we'll get her perspective on your relationship and her upbringing."

"That sounds great," I quickly remembered how getting Khloe to talk to a therapist may be a lot more difficult than we may expect. "Now I just have to see if I can get her in here."

"I'm sure you can manage that job, Dad."

"Let's hope," I said.

"Great," Dr. Turner extended her hand and I shook it graciously. "I'm looking forward to seeing you all next week."

CHAPTER FIVE

The year of 2020...

hat I convinced Khloe to see Dr. Turner, but it was not easy. We did not say much on the ride over because we were both treading in unknown waters. I attempted to be encouraging by telling Khloe that our session was not a psychological analysis of her as my child, but that I would be analyzed as her father. That seemed to relax her a bit. When we entered Dr. Turner's office, Khloe was as expected, nervous and reserved.

"Good afternoon, Dr. Turner," I said.

"Good afternoon, Mr. Simms," Dr. Turner looked at Khloe and smiled, "and you must be Khloe. It is a pleasure to meet you."

"Nice to meet you," Khloe replied.

"Well, have a seat and make yourself comfortable. I promise this'll be like talking to one of your girlfriends," Dr. Turner offered a comforting smile.

"Have a seat, baby," I gestured for Khloe to sit beside me.

Khloe and I sat next to one another, and Dr. Turner smiled and opened the session by directing questions to Khloe.

"I know that seeing a therapist has certain stigmas and stereotypes attached, but I want you to get all of that out of your mind and say whatever you want to say. OK?"

Khloe did not respond. She looked at me and then looked back at Dr. Turner.

"Is everything, OK, sweetheart?"

"Daddy? Would it be alright if I talked to Dr. Turner alone to start off?" Khloe asked reluctantly.

"Sure…sure. That's fine," I turned to Dr. Turner and asked, "is that alright with you, Dr. Turner?"

"That is perfectly fine with me," Dr. Turner answered. "Whatever it takes to make Khloe feel comfortable."

"I'll just be out here waiting on you, OK, babygirl?" I reassured Khloe.

"Daddy, please," Khloe said.

"I'm sorry," I said. "I know you don't like for me to call you that name. But it's just a term of endearment, sweetheart."

"I know, but just…please, don't call me that…ever."

"Alright, alright," I said. "I'm out here if you need me."

"Thank you, Daddy," Khloe smiled, and I knew two things, one, she was beginning to feel comfortable; and two, she really had something that she wanted to share with Dr. Turner.

I walked out of the office and waited anxiously for Khloe in the reception room. Meanwhile, Dr. Turner was working her psychoanalysis magic.

"Now, let's start this all over again," Dr. Turner smiled. "Hi, I'm Dr. Turner. Good to meet you."
"Good to meet you, Dr. Turner. My name is Khloe-Ann Simms but please feel free to call me Khloe. The Ann is not necessary," Khloe joked.

"Khloe? What a pretty name. Once again, I want you to make yourself comfortable and relax. I want you to know that you don't have to say anything you don't want to say. Or, you can tell me everything that's on your mind. But if you feel that you won't be able to tell me everything in the sixty minutes we have today," Dr. Turner joked. "I'll be here next week."

Khloe sat still and quiet with her head down, looking at the floor.

"Are you nervous?" Dr. Turner asked.

"Yes."

"Don't be nervous, Khloe. I'm just here to talk to you, that's all. Nothing you say will leave this room."

"OK," Khloe said.

"Great," Dr. Turner said and then flashed a broad smile. "So, tell me about yourself, Khloe."

Dr. Turner stared at Khloe, waiting for her to speak. Khloe looked up several times wanting to speak. She wanted to say something about the nightmare that had been her life, but she just could not speak.

"It's OK, Khloe. You don't have to rush," Dr. Turner comforted her with another smile. "I want you to go back to your earliest memory of your childhood with your father, mother, school, or…"

"Can I talk about school?" Khloe asked. "Middle school?"

"Absolutely," Dr. Turner nodded. "Let's start from the beginning. How was your first day of school?"

"Actually, I didn't go to school on the first day."

"Really?" Dr. Turner asked, very surprised.

"No," Khloe responded under her breath.

"If you don't mind me asking, why didn't you attend school on the first day?"

"I uh," Khloe became too nervous to speak and lowered her head towards the floor.

"It's OK. You can tell me."

"I... they... I...," Khloe continued to stutter.

"You don't have to talk if you don't feel comfortable,

Khloe.""No, I want to, I just...," Khloe lowered her head

again. "It's OK."

"I actually went to school but...but since I was transferring from another school, my mother had trouble getting me enrolled."

"Oh, OK," Dr. Turner said. "So, who were you referencing earlier when you said, 'they...I...' and all of that?"

"When my mother enrolled me, she saw a few of my friends from my previous school. She was pretty upset because I had gotten in trouble with the same group of girls at my other school."

"What kind of trouble?"

"My friends and I would cut class and hang out at the park, and other places, too. And the truant officer would always catch us wherever we were," Khloe laughed and kept going with her story. "We had fun. We had so much fun that all of us nearly flunked the eighth grade."

"So, your mother decided to separate you girls?"

"Yes," I said. "But my mother didn't know that me and my girls got together behind their backs and came up with this plan to go to a new school. We even added another girl from our crew to join us. Then we would have the entire crew at one school."

"You appear to be very excited talking about your days in middle school?"

"I am very excited," Khloe smiled. "Because that was the only time when I felt like I could be me. At home...at home was pure hell."

"Would you care to explain?"

"Does it stay right here with us?"

"Absolutely." Dr. Turner replied.

"Not even my father will know?"

"No, not even your father will know," Dr. Turner assured. "Whatever you say to me, Khloe, it will stay right here in this office. OK?"

"OK," Khloe paused before continuing, "I used to think there was something wrong with me, Dr. Turner."

"Hmm," Dr. Turner contemplated Khloe's words. "Do you care to explain why you felt that way?"

"Well, it's not that I want something to be wrong with me. My mother used to always tell me that I wanted attention and that's why I acted up, but that wasn't it. I knew that something was wrong with me, and it still is. I just want it fixed so I can be normal."

"You are normal, Khloe. We all have our little quirks that make us a little different from one another. It's just that with some of us it takes a little longer to figure out."

"What exactly do you mean by quirks?" Khloe asked.

"Quirks?" Dr. Turner paused to contemplate how she was going to explain the definition of the word. "Well, it's when we have strange or peculiar habits."

"So you think I'm normal?"

"I ask the questions in this office, young lady," Dr. Turner said sarcastically.

Khloe smiled, but that would be the last significant interaction between them for a while. Khloe and Dr. Turner sat in her office for the next few minutes basically staring at one another. Every now and then Dr. Turner would ask Khloe a question that she felt comfortable answering, and every now and then Khloe would reply with as few words as possible. Although Khloe was still reluctant to share her secrets, Dr. Turner continued to passively urge her to speak freely, until finally Khloe opened up.

"Today I was writing in my journal, or is it a diary?" Khloe asked rhetorically. "Anyway, I was actually typing on my computer, so I was not exactly sure what it is called. Anyway, I have been writing about my personal experiences ever since I was six years old. Growing up in my household with my mother I needed an emotional outlet, and since I had no one else to talk to, I talked to myself. Actually, I wrote to myself. I found my writing to be quite therapeutic. As I grew older and became more computer literate, I took the time to transfer all of the writings of my life from my paper notebooks and saved them on my laptop."

"Interesting," Dr, Turner spoke, "Do you still have those memoirs?"

"Yes, I wanted my previous therapist to look at them, but she wasn't interested."

"Hmm, so this is not your first experience with therapy?"

"No, you are my third."

"But you seemed so uncomfortable earlier."

"It was because I felt like, 'here we go again,' another shrink who's looking to make a buck and not really interested in helping me."

"I guarantee you that I am here to help you," Dr. Turner spoke sincerely, "And I truly apologize for your previous experiences."

"It's not your fault, Dr. Turner. I know that everybody is different."

"Would you like to share your feelings on your perception of therapy?" Dr. Turner asked.

"Well," Khloe sighed. "My first therapist lasted one session. That was it. My second therapist lasted three months, and I think my mental stability worsened."

"So sorry to hear that," Dr. Turner patted Khloe on her hand. "Please, continue."

"After seeing my second therapist for a while, I came to an undeniable conclusion; and that was, my therapist was the one who needed to have her head examined and not me. She literally told me it was all in my head. Can you imagine that? A therapist telling a patient it's all in their head. I wanted to say so badly, 'I know, bitch, and I need you to get it the hell out!' But I didn't. I kept my mouth closed on my final few visits and continued my campaign for a diagnosis of depression. I thought it was important that I find out what the heck was wrong with me. I thought that if I knew what was wrong with me, I could get better," Khloe lowered her head.

"So, tell me, Khloe," Dr, Turner said. "How were things at home?"

"They were OK, I guess."

"OK good or OK bad?"

"Just OK," Khloe answered. "I wanted to move out of my mom's house."

"Why did you want to move out?"

"Because my mother treated me differently from my other sisters because I had a different dad."

"How so?"

"When they would go shopping, I had to stay at home. When it was time to clean up, I had to clean up my room, the kitchen and the living room, while they only had to clean up their rooms and share cleaning up the den."

"Well, how old were they?" Dr. Turner asked.

"One was one year younger than me, and the other was two years older than me. But I did most of the cleaning. I know my mother was getting money from my dad for child support, but her and my stepdad spent most of that money on their kids and very little on me."

"Did you speak to anyone else about this?" Dr. Turner asked.

"Who was I going to talk to, Dr. Turner?"

"A teacher? A counselor? A pastor?" Dr. Turner suggested. "Do you think you could have talked to your dad, Khloe?"

"I didn't officially meet my father until I was seventeen years old, when I enrolled at Spelman University. He somehow found me and brought me to the States. So, all that I had for protection was my mother and stepdad. And trust me, they were as much the enemy as anyone else. I feared living with them."

"You don't have to be afraid of them any longer. If you had a problem with your mom and stepdad, you are allowed to speak your grievances here without judgment or criticism."

"I want to but...," I asked.

"Buuuuuuuut, what?"

"But there are a lot of things that happened to me that my dad does not know."

"That's why you're here, Khloe. To tell me."

"That's easy for you to say. We're safe and sound in your office. I'm the one who is going to have to face my mother and stepdad if my dad finds out. If they treated me mean then, just think how mean they're going to be when they find out I snitched."

"You're not snitching, Khloe. You're telling the truth about being happy or unhappy in your mother's home. That's not snitching. It's telling the truth."

"Where I come from its snitching!"

"So, you would rather remain in an unhappy place than tell the truth?"

"I'm not snitching, Dr. Turner."

"I understand," Dr. Turner nodded and then leaned back. "Is there anything else that went on in your home, other than the cleaning and negligence, that you would like to discuss?"

"No," Khloe paused. "Not really."

"Not really?" Dr. Turner asked. "What else happened, Khloe?"

"I...I...I...," Khloe stuttered.

"What else went on in that home, Khloe?" Dr. Turner repeated more sternly.

"Nothing I couldn't handle, Dr. Turner?" Khloe sighed heavily. "Is my time up?"

"We have plenty of time, Khloe. Talk to me, please. What went on in that house?"

"Nothing!" Khloe shouted.

"OK! OK!" Dr. Turner put her notepad down and sat beside Khloe. "Relax! Relax! We can discuss something else."

Khloe started to cry, "I don't want to talk anymore."

"That's fine," Dr. Turner patted Khloe on the back as she continued to cry. "We don't have to talk anymore. Just relax."

"OK," Khloe wiped her eyes and chuckled, "you're good. I've never cried at a session before."

"I'm simply allowing you a brave space to express yourself."

"Can I continue?"

"Absolutely."

"Well, that was over ten years, and I don't even remember how many sessions, ago. Now when I think about going to my sessions, Dr. Turner, I want to vomit. My dad had to do a lot of convincing to get me here. But it seems with you, I am battling within myself to shut up because of my previous experiences, or to keep talking because I feel comfortable with you." Khloe chuckled.

Dr. Turner returned to her chair and Khloe became her normal talkative self, and Dr. Turner was listening and taking notes as customary. As Khloe began to tell the details of her current affairs, Dr. Turner seemed to be a little distant. Her mind was obviously in another place. Finally, Khloe stopped talking and asked if she was OK.

"Is everything OK, Dr. Turner?"

"Oh, sure. Everything's fine. Why do you ask?"

"You seem to be somewhere else."

"I'm sorry, if I made you feel that way," Dr. Turner adjusted herself in her chair. "I'm listening, please continue."

Dr. Turner patiently sat and listened to Khloe as she went on and on about the depressive points of her life.

"And then there's my boyfriend."

"What about your boyfriend?"

"Well, that's if you want to call him that. Anyway, he was supposed to visit me this past weekend. Well, I waited and waited around for him to show up on Friday. But he was a no-call, no-show. Then I waited all day Saturday and then Saturday night. No-show, no call! I started staring out of my front window waiting for his car to pull up. Nothing! Then I stared at my phone waiting for the phone to ring. Nothing! We were supposed to have gone away for the weekend to take the next step in our relationship."

"What is the next step?" Dr. Turner asked. "Sex?"

"Oh no," Khloe chuckled. "We took that step a long time ago. Our next step was spending quality time together to build on our relationship."

"What do you think happened to your uh…your boyfriend?"

"His wife is what happened."

"His wife?" Dr. Turner seemed surprised by Khloe's response. "Your boyfriend is married?"

"Well…it's a little complicated."

"How complicated is it to say if your boyfriend is married or not married?"

"The complication comes with my boyfriend being separated from his wife."

"So, your boyfriend is married, but separated?"

"Yes," Khloe said.

"And how does that make you feel?"

"Well, it doesn't make me feel

happy."

"OK. Well if it doesn't make you feel happy, then how does it make you feel, Khloe?"

"Disappointed! Used! I don't know," Khloe searched for words but could not find them. "I feel like I've felt my entire life, alone and betrayed."

"Then why do you allow yourself to be in that situation?"

"Because he is there for me?"

"Are you asking me or telling me, Khloe?" Dr. Turner asked.

"I guess I'm telling you," Khloe said. "Anyway, other than my dad, he is the only one that I can trust to be there for me."

"There for you in what capacity?"

"He helps me with my kids. He…he…he helps me with my bills. I can talk to him about anything and he listens. He really puts a smile on my face."

"So, does he make you happy?"

"He does," Khloe nodded her head and smiled as she

responded. "Then where does the sadness come from, Khloe?"

"Because although he's there for me, he's still not entirely my man."

"And how does that make you feel?"

"I want him! I want that man," Khloe paused to compose herself and Dr. Turner passed her a tissue to wipe her eyes. "We have so many, many issues we have to contend with. We are definitely opposites of another. I am an African American, he is white. I am thirty, he is fifty. I am broke, poor, struggling to make it day-to-day. He is wealthy, an entrepreneur and a very important man in the community. With all that being said, we are together but then, we are not."

"How does he feel about your relationship?"

"He tells me he loves me all of the time. But I won't truly believe him until he leaves his wife for good. I deserve to be happy with a man who loves me and only me. You have no idea how many times I fell for these sorry ass men that I have allowed into my lifetime after time after time. I keep being disappointed. But not this time. Not with this man."

"What makes you so certain that this man is different?"

"I don't know." Khloe smiled. "I almost feel as if I can't get this man, then I don't even want to try with another man."

"You're young and you have the rest of your life ahead of you. Are you sure you want to invest so much time and energy into one man?"

"Yes, if it is with the right man."

"Listen, Khloe, I can't tell you what to do, but…,"

Khloe interrupted Dr. Turner very quickly, "Then don't! Please."

"Fine," Dr. Turner said. "Sorry for intruding."

"No need to apologize. As much as I am comfortable about discussing some things, I am equally uncomfortable about discussing other things." Khloe stared at Dr. Turner with complete insecurity and Dr. Turner looked at Khloe with sincere concern. She put her notepad away and removed her eyeglasses from her face. Khloe cleared her throat and began to speak. "I've been taking care of myself my whole life it seems. The fear of falling in love with a man who doesn't love me back is my biggest fear. Because I know how it feels to have a man hurt me. Just once, I want to know what it feels like to have a man truly love me. Just once, Dr. Turner. All the men in my life have always done the same thing to me. Take! Take! Take! Take! Take!"

"What about your dad?"

"All of this stuff that I'm telling you now, my dad doesn't know. My dad could only love me the way he knew how. Not the way I needed. He thinks that my life has been some big ol' fairytale and I let him think that way."

"Why?"

"Because he can't change anything," Khloe sighed heavily. "Fathers can love you unconditionally, but unfortunately, they cannot fix a broken heart."

"I understand," Dr. Turner said. "I can imagine that you may be feeling that the worst thing in the world for a woman is to have her heart broken, but…"

"Don't you feel that way?" Khloe interrupted.

"How I feel is irrelevant, Khloe." Dr. Turner replied. "Now, how do you feel?"

"A broken heart can be mended with time, I guess, but…," Khloe paused.

"But what?" Dr. Turner asked. "I feel that you want to say something, Khloe, but you're having a hard time."

"I'm just thinking," Khloe responded.

"About?"

"About the men in my life."

"Anyone in particular?"

"Not really," Khloe sighed. "I'm just thinking. What did I do as a child for men to feel that they can do whatever they want with me without any repercussions?"

"Would you like to be more specific?"

"Why me, Dr. Turner?" Khloe began to cry while Dr. Turner sat still and waited for her to compose herself. "What is wrong with me that I send out these vibes to men that I want to be stepped on?"

"No one deserves to be stepped on, Khloe, especially you," Dr. Turner walked over to Khloe again and sat beside her. "You have been through a lot in your young lifetime and you have to understand that you are not to blame for what others did to you. Something happened! Tell me…please."

"Nothing happened that I want to discuss," Khloe said shyly.

"I know better than that, Khloe," Dr. Turner wrapped her arm around Khloe's shoulder. "You are under no pressure, but I want you to know, you can talk to me. What happened to you, sweetheart?"

"Well," Khloe paused and looked downward to the floor.

"It's OK, Khloe," Dr. Turner smiled, and Khloe felt comfortable to speak.

"OK," Khloe paused again to contemplate her response and then she prepared to speak. "For almost twenty years I have blocked out a horrible event that happened to me. I mean horrible, horrible event!"

"What happened?" Dr. Turner looked very concerned. "Please explain."

"OK," Khloe said reluctantly. "I'll start from the beginning."

"That's always a good place to start."

"I was born an Army brat on October 20th, 1990 in Tokyo Japan. My mother, Clarice Thomas, was born and raised in a town called Hamilton on the Bermuda Islands. My mother was beautiful, and my father saw that beauty the first time he laid eyes on her. When I was conceived, they were stationed in Japan. He was in the Marine Corps and she was in the Army. My father's deployment was up and he had to return to the United States after a year, so they lost contact. My mother eventually left the Army,

but she wanted me to know my father, so she started to research his career in the Marines. When I was two years old, she was able to locate him in California. She wanted to surprise him with a visit at his military base. Although he was there at the time, we were unable to see him. Two weeks later my father was deployed to Iraq. It was his second deployment to Iraq. He had a six-month stint during the Gulf War a couple of years earlier. It seemed as if my parents were always on two different sides of the globe.

"My mother was very upset with my dad because she thought he should have tried to find his child. After my mother was discharged from the Army, we relocated to Texas for a little while. That was where she met my stepfather, who was also a Bermudian. He convinced my mother to move to his hometown of St. George, so that's how we returned home to Bermuda. Ironically, my father had been searching for us the entire time. By the time he found us in Texas, my mother was engaged, and we were preparing to relocate back to Bermuda. She secretly met with my dad and he saw me for the first time. Of course, I was too young to remember that day. He drove all the way from California to Texas just to see me. Unfortunately, I did not see my father again until I was seventeen years old.

"When I was sixteen, I received a message from my father on Facebook stating who he was and that he wanted to talk to me. I was apprehensive at first. For all I knew, he could have been some pervert trying to seduce me into a sex traffic scandal. Eventually, I talked to my mother and she confirmed that he was indeed my father. The first thing I wanted to know was where the hell he had been all of that time? He apologized and he explained that he had been trying to find me for years. He also told me that he had made contact with my mother and stepfather to talk to me. He said he gave them his contact information, but they never relayed the message to me. I was furious with my mother. I never cared much for my stepfather anyway. After talking it over with my father, we decided that after I graduated from high school, I would attend college at Spelman University where he lived.

"During my freshman year, I became pregnant and had to drop out of school for a while. My father could have come down hard on me, but he didn't. He was patient and understanding. I don't think he was very happy about becoming a grandfather in his early forties, but he made sure that I knew that he was going to have my back no matter what happened. I was blessed to have my son Chaz who's now three years old. I am also blessed to have two younger sisters as babysitters," Khloe joked.

"Is there anything else you would like to share?" Dr. Turner asked.

"Actually, there is...,"

—

When I was twelve years old, I lived in St. George, a town on the island of Bermuda, with my mother. But then I went to spend the summer with my aunts in Memphis, Tennessee, here in the United States. My younger siblings were back home in Bermuda. I was so excited to be around my real family and not my stepdad's family. My aunts promised my mother that they would take good care of me and try to lead me back in the right direction. There was nothing wrong with me except I wanted to be treated the same as my sisters, but my stepfather was not a fan of that. He just wanted to create a valid reason to get me out of his house until I could "get better." That's the same thing we called it when my mother was going through her drug thing, "getting better."

Anyway, when I first got to my Aunties' houses it was strange at first. I wasn't used to that part of Memphis. They lived in the southside of Memphis, which was still much, much larger than the entire island of Bermuda. It was also much more dangerous.

I received a lot of attention from my cousins and both of my Aunties. My Auntie Trisha lived a couple houses down from Auntie Jean. I had three female cousins that were close to my age. Tammy was fourteen. She was Auntie Trisha's daughter. Gloria, who we called Glow, was fifteen. Freda, whose nickname was Frenchy, was the oldest and she was sixteen. Glow and Frenchy were Auntie Jean's daughters. I followed them everywhere.

There was something to do every day. Our favorite places to go were the skating rink and the mall. We met a lot of boys during that summer. A lot of boys! They were all older than me. Not just me, they were older than all of us. Both of my Aunties worked third shift at the same bottling plant, so we had all kinds of fun. Tammy stayed at Auntie Jean's house with us while Auntie Trisha was at work.

One night they decided to let some of their friends come over-- John, Money, Ranch and Boney. They were much older than us. John was eighteen. Money was nineteen. Ranch was seventeen and Boney was seventeen. I had met them before, but it was always at the mall or at the skating rink. They were brothers and hoodlums to the tenth power, but they were also kind of fun.

I sat in the living room watching television while they were in the kitchen. The boys had brought something to drink with them. I do not know what it was because it was in a brown bag. But whatever it was, they were passing it around to one another. Which made me assume that it was liquor. They made sure I only came into the kitchen to go to the bathroom and then they rushed me back into the living room.

Around ten o'clock, I became sleepy and I stretched out on the couch. I fell asleep quickly and then I heard the shuffling of people going in and out of the door. I kept dozing in and out as folks constantly walked past. I was awakened by Frenchy shaking me rather vigorously.

"Hey!" Frenchy said. "John 'bout to run us to the store right quick. Money is gon' stay here with you until we get back."

I did not think anything of it, and I went back to sleep. Auntie Jean's couch was kind of small so I would sleep with my face facing the couch so my backside could hang off of the couch. I usually bunked on the couch, so I was getting used to it. I was small and did not take up much space. I was about five-feet even at that time and I weighed maybe ninety pounds soaking wet. While I was sleeping, I started to feel my body move involuntarily. At first, I was afraid because I didn't know what was happening. Then I could see that Money was sitting on the edge of the couch next to me. He was rubbing my leg beneath the covers. I pretended to be sleep as he rubbed my legs up and down. He started to breathe harder and harder and I kept pretending to be asleep. I started to pray that Frenchy and the girls would hurry up and come back.

My hair was in ponytails most of the time but when it was straightened that night, I suppose I looked very mature for a twelve-year-old. I certainly received my fair share of glances from the older boys. I had nice brown eyes and a cute pointed nose. My body was slender, or what some may call petite, yet curvaceous for a twelve-year-old. I had smooth, unblemished skin that was often complimented. I had been told throughout my life that I had an infectious smile, but that night I regretted it all. I slept in my mother's nightgown. It was sentimental, old and most importantly, unwittingly provided problematic easy access to my private parts.

Money tried to slide his hands inside of my panties, but all of the pockets of my gown would not allow him to do that. He stood up and pulled down his pants. I started to cry and continued to pray. He kneeled beside me and moved closer and closer until I could feel him pressed against my backside. I did not move because I was pretending to be asleep. He reached his arm around my waist and pulled me backwards into him. He moved his hips towards me and started to grind himself against me. I was so close to the big, fluffy pillows that lined the back of the couch that my face was nearly touching them. The closer I moved to the back of the couch the closer Money moved towards me. My face was literally pressed against those huge pillows on that couch, and it was difficult for me to breathe.

"Khloe?" Money whispered. I ignored him, hoping it would deter him from trying to wake me. But he only repeated himself and nudged me. "Khloe?"

"Huh?" I responded weakly, hoping he would think that I slept through all of it.

"You woke?"

"Naw," I yawned to try to make the point that I was indeed asleep.

"Wake up."

"I'm sleepy, Mr. Money."

"I ain't old enough to be called no mister, Khloe."

I turned my head sideways so that he could hear me clearly, "Money, I don't know what you trying to do but Frenchy and 'nem gon' be back real soon. Please let me go back to sleep. I know we told y'all I was fifteen but I'm only twelve. If you do something with me, you might get in a lot of trouble."

"I ain't gon' get in trouble because we ain't gon' do nothing wrong," Money started to pull my covers down.

"You gon' get in trouble if you mess with me!" I said, as I pulled my covers all the way up to my neck. "I'm gon' tell my Auntie, just leave me alone."

"What yo' Auntie gon' do?" Money laughed. "I ain't did nothing to you. And I ain't gon' do nothin' to you. I'm just asking you some questions, that's all."

"I felt you touching on my legs, Money, and I'm gon' tell my Auntie if you don't leave me alone!"

Money grabbed me by the back of my gown and snatched me onto the floor. He wrapped his hands around my neck and choked me. I tried to remove his hands, but he was much too strong.

"What's gon' happen is, you gon' mess around and get you, your cousins and your Aunties killt!" Money shouted. He wrapped his hands tighter around my throat and pressed down. "Now you ain't gon' tell nobody nothin' is you?"

I could not talk. I could only shake my head from side to side. He leaned down and kissed me. I did not show much resistance and I kissed him back as best I knew how. I was twelve and had never kissed anyone, so I did what I had seen on television. He seemed to be enjoying it but I was sick. His body felt heavy on top of me. He took his right leg and tried to separate both of mine. I tried to keep my legs together. I withstood him for as long as I could, but he was too powerful. He lifted my gown and played with my chest very aggressively. I remember how rough his hands felt groping me. He panted loudly as his hands moved downward to my panties. I stopped him momentarily by putting my hands between his hands and my private parts. Then he began to choke me again. Fortunately, the headlights from the car my cousins were riding in shined in the house and he released his grip on my neck.

"Now you bet' not say a word when they get in here 'cause if you do I'm killin' all y'all! You hear me?" Money said with a menacing frown on his face.

I nodded yes.

"Now get yo' ass back on that couch and act like you sleep."

I climbed back on the couch and covered my head. My cousins and their friends marched into the house giggling. They had no idea what their friend Money had just done to me and I was too afraid to tell them. Frenchy, who always played mother hen to the rest of us, came to check on me.

"You sleep?" Frenchy asked.

I continued to face the back of the couch and did not turn around to face her. She pulled me around to her and looked at me.

"Hey, you OK?"

I nodded yes, and then I covered up my head again.

"Yo, hey," Frenchy said. "Did anything happen while we was gone?"

I thought about the threat Money had made to me and I lied. I didn't want anything to happen to me or my family. "No. I'm just sleepy that's all.'"

"You   sure?"

"Yeah, I'm sure."

Frenchy kissed me on my forehead and went into the kitchen with the rest of her friends. Frenchy was a girl, but she was a tough girl. The boys in the neighborhood didn't even mess with her. There was only one person that she said she would not try, and it was Money. Money had a reputation for being crazy. Rumor was that he had killed a couple of boys down there in Hamilton. Hamilton is the capital city of Memphis. Although I wanted to tell Frenchy what had happened, I thought that if I did, she would have said something to Money, and he would have

killed all of us. I was just happy that the nightmare was over, but then the next thing I knew Money whispered in my ear, "You bet' not tell nobody!"

And I didn't! I kept it to myself. From that night on, when we went around Money, I never said a word. I kept my head down and kept my mouth shut.

CHAPTER SIX

The summer of 2002...

One night I was sitting in Auntie Jean's house and Frenchy, Glow and Tammy were outside with John, Ranch and Boney. They were making a lot of noise but that was nothing new. Every night was a party at Auntie Jean's house. While I was sitting on the couch, Money came through the back door and snuck up behind me.

"Hey," Money whispered. "c'mere."

"For what?" I asked defiantly.

"Just come here."

"I...uh...I can't," I said nervously.

"Girl, you better bring your ass on out this back do'!"

I looked at the front door, waiting for someone to walk through and save me, but they didn't. Money grabbed me by the hand and led me out of the back door onto the porch. As soon as the door closed, he pushed me against the door and immediately put his hands between my legs.

"Money, please, stop!"

"Why?" Money moaned.

"'Cause you hurting me!" I tried to slide away from him, but he pulled me back and I could not move at all. "Stop it!"

"It's OK. I'm not gon' hurt you," Money grinded on my thigh while he was rubbing between my legs.

"STOP IT!'" I screamed as loud as I could. Then all of a sudden, the noise stopped from the front of the house. Money pushed me against the house and grabbed me by the throat. He started to make a grunting noise that I could not understand. He was livid. He frowned and punched the house directly to the side of my head.

"I'll kill you! I'll kill you! I'll kill you!" Money grunted. "You hear me?"

I covered my face to protect myself and hoped he didn't hit me. I turned my back to him and began to cry. He offered no sympathy for me at all. Instead he grabbed me by the arms and shoved me against the house several times. We could hear people running in the house towards the back door. Money looked through the screen door and then zipped up his pants.

"I'm telling you, if you tell anybody I was here, you dead, and your whole family dead, you hear me?" Money snarled and that turned into a mean grin.

Money jumped off of the porch and disappeared in the darkness. By that time, Frenchy and the others were bursting through the back door.

"What's wrong with you?" Frenchy yelled.

"I thought I heard somebody out here and when I came out here, they ran over that way," I pointed towards some tall bushes in the opposite direction that Money ran.

"You saw somebody where?" Glow asked.

"Over there by them bushes," I answered.

"Ain't nothing over there by them bushes, Khloe!" Tammy snapped.

"I know what I saw!" I snapped back.

"Wait a minute," John bent down and picked up a baseball cap lying on the ground, "Is this one of y'all's cap?"

"Not mine," Frenchy said.

"Not mine, either," Glow said.

"I don't even live here," Tammy said.

"I'm thinking that cap belongs to whoever Khloe heard out here on this porch," Boney said.

"Stop trying to scare people, Boney," Frenchy said.

"I ain't trying to scare nobody, Frenchy," Boney said. "But if that ain't one of y'all's cap, who cap is it?"

I listened to everything everybody was saying, and I didn't say a word. I kept my mouth shut like Money had told me.

"Wait, I know who cap that is," John said.

"Who cap is it?" Frenchy asked

I was hoping John kept his big mouth shut. But he didn't.

That's Money's cap," John said.

"Money?" Frenchy asked. "You sure this Money's cap?"

"Yeah, I'm sure that's my brother's cap," John reached for the cap. "Give it to me."

"I ain't giving you nothing!" Frenchy said as she snatched the cap away. "If your brother want this cap, tell him to come get it!"

"Hey, don't be crazy, Frenchy," John said, "I'm trying to stop you from getting yourself in trouble now. Gimme' the dam cap before that nigga come back and get it himself."

"You might want to give him the hat, Frenchy," Boney said. "Money crazy as hell. Ain't no telling what he'll do to y'all if he finds out you holding on to his cap 'cause you think he was creeping around your house."

"I ain't scared of no Money! He can die just like anybody else can die."

Ranch, who was always quiet, finally spoke up, "Who's going to kill him, Frenchy? You?" Ranch pointed at Frenchy. "You better give us that cap and act like this night never happened. I know my brother, and he ain't going back to jail and he don't mind killing nobody to stay free."

"Right!" Boney said. "Gimme' the cap, Frenchy."

"Give 'em the cap, Frenchy," Glow said.

"Why?" Frenchy shouted. "That fool was sniffin' around our house and now we gon' act like we scared of him? My mama ain't raise no punk!"

"You ain't no punk, Frenchy. But don't be stupid either. Money don't give a dam about none of us! I don't know why you making a big deal over that funky ol' cap anyway! Give it to 'em so they can go!" Glow said.

"No!" Frenchy said stubbornly and then looked at me. "What happened out here on this porch, Khloe?"

I didn't know whether I should be more afraid of Money or Frenchy at that point. I looked down at the ground and didn't respond. Frenchy walked over to me and raised my head. "Now I'm going to ask you one mo' time, Khloe. What happened out here on this porch?"

"Nothing," I said.

"Was Money out here on this porch?" Frenchy shouted.

"No!" I said while lowering my head.

"Are you lying to me?"

"No!" I tried to walk back in the house, but Frenchy grabbed me.

"Listen to me, Khloe!" Frenchy shouted again. "You don't have to be scared of no nigga! If he did something to you, tell me!"

"Nobody did nothing to me," I said nervously.

"Hey, y'all get away from my house!" Frenchy said to John, Boney and Ranch.

"Frenchy, would you please give us that cap?" Ranch said.

"Man, y'all ain't getting' shit! Now get away from my house!"

"Give us the gotdam cap!" John shouted.

"OK, you want a cap?" Frenchy started to walk into the house. "I'll give you a cap alright. I'll bust a cap in all yo' ass! Stay right here till I get back!"

"Man, that fool crazy!" Boney shouted.

Frenchy ran into the house and John, Ranch and Boney ran away from the house. Frenchy returned with an old gun in her hand that probably didn't work, looking for the brothers. "Where they at?"

"They gone!" Glow said.

"They better be gone!" Frenchy lowered the gun to the ground. "They think 'cause we females they just gon' come take over our house. Ain't nobody comin' up in this house disrespecting us!"

We followed Frenchy back into the house and she was on alert for the remainder of the night, until Auntie Jean came home from work. I thought when she told Auntie Jean what had happened, that Auntie Jean was going to go off on Frenchy for getting that gun, but instead she reinforced to her that she had done the right thing. Apparently, the leaf did not fall too far from the tree. Auntie Jean was notorious in their neighborhood for being a tough no-nonsense single mother.

—

One Sunday afternoon, Auntie Jean and Auntie Trisha were at church and Frenchy, Glow and Tammy were at Auntie Jean's house. I had wandered down to Auntie Trisha's house to play in Tammy's old tree house. I was playing with her dolls when I heard someone climbing up the stairs. I had just sat down, so I assumed whoever it was must have followed me from Auntie Jean's house. The stairs leading to the treehouse were old and wooden. They creaked and swayed whenever someone stepped on them. One by one, I slowly heard the sound of someone walking up the stairs. I stopped playing with the dolls and stared at the curtain covering the door. My instincts were sensing that something was wrong. The curtain slowly peeled back and Money stepped in with a broad sinister smile on his face.

"How you doing, babygirl?" Money asked.

I didn't respond. I tried to run around him, but he grabbed me and threw me to the floor. He forced himself on top of me, and we were face to face. I could smell his terrible alcoholic breath. He looked me in my eyes and roughly held my face in his hands. I closed my eyes and he started to pull his pants down. I started to cry, but he wouldn't stop. He kissed me gently on my left cheek, and then softly on the right. I kept my eyes shut tightly hoping the monster would go away. He reached between us and unbuttoned my pants. He snatched my pants down and opened up my legs with his legs. I didn't even try to resist or fight back, because I knew I could not stop him, and I did not want to make him angry. I just wanted it to be over as quickly as possible. He pulled my panties to the side and plunged himself inside of me with brute force. It was the most excruciating pain I had ever felt in my life. I tried to close my thighs, but it was as if his legs had superhuman strength. He rammed me over and over and over until he moaned loudly and collapsed on top of me.

He panted wildly, trying to catch his breath. My entire body was numb and sore. I suppose I was still crying but I couldn't hear myself. I just wanted him off of me and away from me. He rolled over and started to pull his pants up.

"See," Money said as he was still trying to catch his breath. "That wasn't too bad, was it, baby girl?"

All of a sudden, the curtain flew back and Frenchy burst in with that gun in her hand, "I told you the last time you put your nasty hands on me that that was the last time I was going to let you get away with that shit."

"Put that gun down, Frenchy," Money said.

"Get outta' here, Khloe!" Frenchy shouted.

Frenchy helped me pull my clothes up as she held the gun pointed at Money. Although I was disoriented, I managed to walk to the door where Tammy and Glow were waiting for me. They helped me down the stairs. When we reached the bottom step, we heard one loud pop. When we looked up, Frenchy poked her head outside of the curtain and said calmly, "One of y'all better call 911."

I don't know who called the police, but they were notified. Tammy and Glow were on either side of me and practically carried me all the way to my Auntie Jean's house. They took me to the bathroom and started to wash me. I could hear the sound of sirens growing louder and louder as they came closer to the house. I was simultaneously afraid and confused. I think I was just as afraid of the police as I was of Money.

"Is the police coming to get me?" I asked nervously.

"No baby," Glow said. "Ain't nobody coming to get

you." "We got to get you clean, that's all," Tammy added.

"What did that fool do to you?" Glow asked.

I took a moment to think of what Glow was asking me. I suppose the reality of my traumatic experience with Money hit me all at once. I thought about Money threatening me! I thought about Money choking me! I thought about…I thought about Money raping me. I looked at Glow and then I looked at Tammy. I couldn't respond. I shook my head slowly from side to side. Then I shook my head faster and faster.

"Hey!" Glow said. "Hey! You OK?"

"I think she's going into shock, Glow!" Tammy yelled.

"Be quiet. You're scaring her. You don't even know what shock is, Tammy," Glow snapped.

My body became numb and my mind started to swirl all over the place. I became flooded with emotions and I lost it. I dropped to the floor of the bathroom. I screamed to the top of my lungs and pounded my fists against the wall. It was as if all of the fear that I had inside of me suddenly left and it was replaced with raging anger.

"I hate him! I hate him! I hate him!" I screamed.

"Shh! Shhhhhhhhh!" Glowed hugged me and Tammy restrained my arms. "Calm down, Khloe, calm down."

"Why that man do this to me?" I cried. "Why?"

"It's OK!" Glow said as she rocked me back and forth.

"We got to get you clean," Tammy said.

"I don't think we need to clean her down there until we take her to the hospital," Glow insisted.

"Let's just wash her face then. We can't have her lookin' like this," Tammy added.

"OK," Glow said as she was trying to hold me up.

I had spent so much energy that I became totally exhausted. My body went limp and Glow and Tammy tried to attach my clothes, so that most of my body was not revealed. I just laid there and let them do what they had to do. It didn't matter if they cleaned me or not. They could have washed my body 'til the cows came home, and I still wouldn't have felt clean. I felt dirty! I felt violated! No amount of soap and water in the world could have made me feel clean that day.

As Glow and Tammy were fixing my clothes, Auntie Jean and Auntie Trisha rushed in the house. We heard them coming towards the bathroom and then they burst through the door.

"We got a call at the church to come home…," Auntie Trisha looked at me and stopped in mid-sentence, "what the hell?"

"What happened to her?" Auntie Jean asked.

Tammy and Glow looked back and forth at one another and Auntie Jean screamed very loudly, "I said, WHAT HAPPENED TO HER?"

"Um," Glow said, "A boy named Money raped her."

"What?" Auntie Trisha asked in disbelief.

"Who raped who now?" Auntie Jean asked as she went into the bedroom.

"A boy named Money raped Khloe, Ma," Glow said.

"Where's my gun?" Auntie Jean screamed from her bedroom.

"What happened?" Auntie Trisha asked again.

Auntie Jean walked back to the bathroom door with her hands on her hips and asked very politely, "Where the hell is my gun?"

"Frenchy got it," Glow said.

"Where can I find this Money boy?" Auntie Jean asked as she ransacked her room still looking for her gun that we had just told her was in Frenchy's possession.

"Don't get too excited, sister. Let's find out what happened first," Auntie Trisha said.

"I'm not excited…I'm not excited," Auntie Jean mumbled. "That's exactly what I'm going to do. Find out what happened."

"I just…can somebody please tell me what happened?" Auntie Trisha pleaded but before anyone could reply, Auntie Jean walked back to the bathroom's doorway.

"Where is Frenchy?" Auntie Jean asked.

"Y'all didn't see all those police cars in front of your house, Auntie Trisha?" Glow asked.

"I wasn't paying any attention to no police. They're in front of my house almost every day."

"What do those police have to do with Frenchy?" Auntie Jean asked.

"Frenchy shot Money up in Tammy's old tree house," Glow said.

"What did she say?" Auntie Trisha asked as she looked over at Auntie Jean.

"Now you can tell me to calm down," Auntie Jean said to Auntie Trisha.

Auntie Jean stormed out of the house.

"Listen, don't touch that girl! Leave her like she is until the police check her out," Auntie Trisha advised.

Auntie Trisha left in a rush to try to catch up with Auntie Jean. Auntie Jean and Auntie Trisha started off walking sort of cautiously, but as they grew closer to Auntie Trisha's house, they picked up their pace. By that time, plenty of neighbors had come out of their homes and surrounded Auntie Trisha's house. The police detained my Aunties as they walked across the lawn to Auntie Trisha's house.

"I'm sorry, ladies. I'm Detective Riley. This is a crime scene so you're going to have to stand back, ma'am," Detective Riley said.

"I live here, officer, and I'm looking for my niece," Auntie Trisha said.

Auntie Jean paid no attention to the officer and kept running across the lawn towards the back of the house.

"Ma'am! Ma'am!" Detective Riley yelled to Auntie Jean. He then turned to Auntie Trisha and said, "You stay here!"

The police officer pursued Auntie Jean, but before he could catch up with her, she was subdued by two other police officers. They held her by her arms on either side until Detective Riley walked in front of her.

"Ma'am! Ma'am! We can't let you go up in that tree!" Detective Riley shouted.

"My daughter is up in that tree!"

"No, no she's not, ma'am."

"Where is she?" Auntie Jean screamed.

"She's at the station, ma'am," Detective Riley said. "She's fine. We just have to ask her a few questions. If you'd like, I can have a car run you to the station."

"Take me to my child!" Auntie Jean said as she composed herself.

"Hey!" Detective Riley waved a uniformed officer over.

"Yeah?" the officer said, with a confused look on his face.

"Run these ladies to the station. They're the mother and auntie of the girl."

"Sure," the officer said. "Come with me, ladies."

"I, uh, I think I need to stay here and check on the girls," Auntie Trisha said.

"OK," Auntie Jean said as she quickly walked off with the officer.

As Detective Riley started to walk away, Auntie Trisha called him, "Uh, Detective Riley?"

"Yes, ma'am?"

"How's the boy?" Auntie Trisha asked.

"I'm afraid he didn't make it, ma'am."

As Detective Riley was speaking, a police officer started to mark off the crime scene with yellow tape. Auntie Trisha stepped back as the officer moved in front of her.

"Is he still up there?" Auntie Trisha asked.

"Yes ma'am."

Auntie Trisha covered her mouth and started to cry. She walked off with tears flowing more and more. By the time she arrived back to Auntie Jean's house, two female police officers were taking me to the hospital to be examined. Auntie Trisha stopped us on the way to the police car. Tammy and Glow were with me.

"Hey! Hey! Hey!" Auntie Trisha walked towards the police car. "Excuse me, officers, where are you taking my girls?"

"Good afternoon, ma'am, I'm Officer Collins," Officer Collins, a masculine looking female, shook Auntie Trisha's hand. "Are you the mother of the alleged victim?"

"No, I'm her auntie."

"I'm Officer Reed," Officer Reed, a much more feminine looking woman, shook Auntie Trisha's hand. "We're about to take your niece to the hospital for an examination."

"I would like to go with her," Auntie Trisha said.

"You're perfectly welcome to follow us, ma'am," Officer Reed responded.

"Y'all come with me," Auntie Trisha started to walk towards her car and we started to follow her until Officer Collins stopped us.

"No! No! No! No! No!" Officer Collins said to me. "You have to come with us, sweetheart."

I didn't know whether to go with the police officers or follow my auntie.

"Go with them, baby, I'll be right behind you," Auntie Trisha reassured me.

"OK," I walked over to the police car, and the officers opened the door for me to get in and then closed it behind me. I was scared to death. I had never been in a police car before. I stared at Auntie Trisha, Glow and Tammy as we pulled away.

The two officers talked to one another on the way to the hospital, but they didn't say a word to me. We pulled into the rear entry of the hospital. I guess that was the entrance police officers used, because it certainly wasn't a public area. They took me to a small room and a nurse walked in and started to ask me questions. By that time, my Auntie Trisha, Tammy and Glow walked in the room. Officer Collins, who was standing near the door, would not allow all of them into the room.

"Excuse me," Officer Collins said. "Only one of you can be in here with Khloe at a time. Ma'am, you can stay, but the girls are going to have to wait in the waiting room."

"Y'all heard her," Auntie Trisha said, "Go down there to the waiting room."

"OK," Glow looked at me. "You OK?"

I nodded my head.

"I'll see you when they get done," Tammy said.

I nodded my head again. When Glow and Tammy walked out, the nurse started to run tests on me. My Auntie Trisha held my hand the entire time. She was trying to hold back her tears and not show me that she was crying, but I could see. When the nurse finished with my exam, Officer Collins asked my auntie to step outside the room to talk to her. As I was putting on my clothes, I could hear their conversation.

"Well, we are a little concerned about your niece," Officer Collins said.

"So am I," Auntie Trisha said.

"I'm sorry, ma'am, I mean we're concerned about your niece's allegations that she was actually raped."

"What do you mean?" Auntie Trisha slightly raised her voice. I was surprised because Auntie Trisha was always mild-mannered and soft-spoken. In total contrast to Auntie Jean, who was sharp-tongued and outspoken.

"I mean that your niece is not exhibiting the behavior of someone who was just raped, especially for a twelve-year-old child."

"Is there a specific way that she is supposed to act?"

"Not specifically, but she seems rather composed and nonchalant to have just experienced such a traumatic incident."

"You ever think that maybe she's reacting to the traumatic experience because she was actually traumatized?"

"It's my job to get to the bottom of the truth, ma'am," Officer Collins said cynically. "That means I have to investigate all of the different scenarios."

"My niece was raped!" Auntie Trisha snapped.

"And a young man is dead!" Officer Collins snapped back.

Until I heard Officer Collins mention Money's death outside of my hospital room, it had not dawned on me that Frenchy had actually killed him. I heard the gunshot, but I didn't put two-and-two together that someone would die. At that point, I just wanted to go home. Right then and there! I wanted to go back to St. George with my dysfunctional family and forget all about Memphis, Tennessee.

"I am sorry for that young man," Auntie Trisha lowered her voice. "I guess I'm trying to deal with this the best way I know how, because nothing like this has ever happened to me, especially at my house. I have a young man dead in my backyard. I have a niece in the hospital that has just been raped. And I have a niece at the police station being questioned for murder. So, forgive me if I am not in the most courteous of moods right now."

"First of all, ma'am, your niece is not being questioned for murder. Your niece admitted to shooting another person and she is being questioned for details. I am sorry that all of this has happened to you all at once, but I am simply trying to do my job."

"I know," Auntie Trisha said apologetically. "I'm sorry."

"I understand," Officer Collins smiled. "I think your niece could probably use a hug."

"I think so, too."

I sat up straight as I heard Auntie Trisha walking back into the room. She walked over and gave me a tight hug. She lifted up my face and kissed me on the cheek.

"I love you, little girl," Auntie Trisha said.

"I love you, too, auntie," I said.

"I am so, so sorry this happened to you, Khloe."

I lowered my head and Auntie Trisha put her arms around my shoulders, and we walked back to the waiting room where Tammy and Glow were waiting for us. They asked me about the tests, but I really didn't talk much. I either nodded my head, yes, or I shook my head, no, to their questions. When we got into the car, Auntie Trisha made them stop asking me questions and leave me alone.

It was almost dark when we got back home, and Auntie Jean and Frenchy were still at the police station. I lay on the couch with my head in Glow's lap. She braided my hair as I watched television. Every now and then she would rub the side of my face. She would ask me if I was OK periodically, and I would nod my head, yes.

Although they had removed Money's body from the tree house, Auntie Trisha and Tammy were still too afraid to sleep at their house, so they decided to sleep at Auntie Jean's house with us. It was a very strange feeling in the house that night. No one could sleep and no one wanted to talk. Well, I wanted to sleep but every time I closed my eyes, I saw Money on top of me and then I would imagine Frenchy shooting him with that gun. Tammy and Glow slept in the living room with me that night. I kept waking up throughout the night screaming in terror. I felt bad for keeping them up, but I couldn't stop thinking about Frenchy and Money. Around two o'clock in the morning, the front door opened, and Auntie Jean walked in. My heart started to beat fast because Frenchy was not behind her. What seemed like forever passed, and then Frenchy slowly walked in the house. I sat up straight and ran to her.

"You, OK?" Frenchy asked.

I nodded my head, yes. Auntie Jean didn't say much when she came in. She went straight to her room and closed the door. From under the door I could see she had her lamp on, so I assumed she was reading her Bible like she always did. I followed Frenchy around for the remainder of the night. When she took a shower, I sat on the floor outside of the bathroom door. After she finished her shower, she opened the door and I fell backwards onto the bathroom floor. She laughed and helped me to my feet. She held my hand and led me to the living room where Tammy and Glow had finally fallen asleep. I sat on the couch next to Frenchy and again she asked me, "You OK?"

Again, I nodded my head, yes. I wanted to ask Frenchy what happened at that police station, but I still couldn't speak. When I said I couldn't speak, I mean, I had the ability to speak. I just didn't have the will. Luckily, Frenchy took it upon herself to tell me.

"You've been kinda' close to me ever since me and mama got back, Khloe. I don't want you worrying about me, OK?"

I nodded my head, yes.

"I ain't in no trouble. Ranch came to the police station and told them what happened to you back there on that porch. You ain't the only one Money did that to, and the police know it. I told him. I told him...," Frenchy paused and then shook her head in sadness. "I told him to get up off of you. And then he tried to come at me. So, I shot him! So, they let me go! I guess they say it's self-defense. Anyway, you don't have to worry about him. And you don't have to worry about me. OK?"

I smiled and nodded my head, yes. I tried to speak with all of the power of my voice, but unfortunately, I could not.

"I know you're spooked by all of this, but I hate to tell you, it's life. We weren't born in the perfect family, to go to the perfect schools, live in the perfect neighborhood, and to live a perfect life. This is the life that we got, and we got to get through it the best way we know how. So, when shit like this happen, you got two choices, you can fight or flight. I don't know about you, but I ain't runnin' from no gotdam body," Frenchy said. "You feel me?"

Once again, I nodded yes.

CHAPTER SEVEN

The summer of 2002...

The next few weeks were pure hell. Although the police said Frenchy killed Money in self-defense, they kept coming around the house asking questions. Frenchy didn't care about the police and she didn't back down. She showed no remorse, and that almost got her in trouble one afternoon when Detective Riley stopped by to talk to her and she practically told him that she was glad she killed Money.

Frenchy, Tammy, Glow and I were sitting on the porch when Detective Riley pulled up. He stopped the car and looked at us before getting out. He waved while still sitting in the car. He exited the car and then started walking towards us. Frenchy rolled her eyes and sighed heavily.

"I can't stand this man!" Frenchy sighed.

"How are you young ladies today?" Detective Riley smiled.

"I'm fine," Glow said.

"I'm good," Tammy said.

I lowered my head and didn't say a word.

"How are you doing, young lady?" Detective Riley said to me directly.

I waved at him and kept my head down. I assumed he had stopped by because he was concerned about me being raped. The tests had come back and confirmed that I had indeed been raped and from the result of that rape, I suffered from RTS, or Rape Traumatic Syndrome. Officer Collins had even made a special trip to Auntie Jean's house to talk and to console me. I thanked her with a smile, but I really didn't have anything more to offer her at that time. However, I respectfully listened to her.

So, as I said, I assumed Detective Riley had stopped by for the same reason as Officer Collins. But after speaking to me, Detective Riley turned all of his attention back to Frenchy. She was not in a very friendly mood.

"So, uh, is Frenchy your birth name?"

"Why?" Frenchy said with an attitude. "You know my name."

"You might want to fix that attitude, young lady."

"I ain't got no attitude," Frenchy snapped.

"Just answer my questions," Detective Riley said.

"Answer my question!" Frenchy said. "Why do you y'all keep coming around here every single day asking me questions? They said it was self-defense so leave me alone!"

"I'm not so sure about that, Frenchy," Detective Riley said.

"Well I am!"

"What um," Detective Riley kneeled in front of Frenchy's face, "What really happened in that tree house, Frenchy?"

"I got Money up off my baby cousin. That's what happened in that tree house."

"Was it premeditated?" Detective Riley asked.

"How do I premeditate a rape?" Frenchy asked sarcastically. "I ain't got no da…"

Detective Riley interrupted Frenchy, "You watch your mouth! You knew your cousin was in that tree house all the time, didn't you?"

"Yeah, that's why I went up there."

"I know you did. But you also knew Money was in that tree house, didn't you?"

"And?" Frenchy asked with attitude.

"And what took you so long to climb up in that tree house to save your cousin, Frenchy?"

"What?" Frenchy realized that Detective Riley wasn't just antagonizing her. He was trying to coerce her into admitting that when she shot Money it was premeditated murder. "What you trying to say?"

"You knew Money was up in that tree with your cousin. Why did you stand by and wait for him to rape her before you stopped him?"

"Man, you talking crazy!" Frenchy shouted.

"Am I?" Detective Riley shouted back. "If you cared so much about your cousin, why did you let that boy rape her, Frenchy? Answer my question!"

"Frenchy didn't know Money was in that tree until I heard Khloe screaming. And then I ran and got her!" Tammy shouted.

Frenchy was so mad that her chest was heaving up and down and she was breathing heavily through her nose like a raging bull. I knew she was about to explode. However, surprisingly, she was able to maintain her composure until she sent me in the house.

"Khloe! Go in the house!" Frenchy said.

150

I didn't hesitate to move. I jumped up from the stairs and ran in the house. I didn't go far though. I stood to the side, inside of the screen door, so that I could still hear.

"Now what you say?" Frenchy stood up and looked Detective Riley in the face.

"What happened in that tree house, Frenchy?" Detective Riley repeated.

"Money raped my cousin and I killed him! If any other man mess with me or my family, I'm gon' kill they ass, too."

"That's what I thought," Detective Riley smiled sinisterly.

"Y'all can keep on sending different people around here every day, if you want to. I ain't scared 'cause the truth ain't gon' change," Frenchy shouted. "You think I don't remember? Huh? You think I don't know that you used to work in Vice, Detective Riley? Huh? You think I don't know who you are? Stop acting like you care about what happens in the hood! You don't care! You only snooping around here now 'cause Money was yo' nephew!"

"You best shut yo' mouth, girl," Detective Riley grunted.

"I ain't shuttin' shit. It's time for you to answer my questions," Frenchy walked off of the porch and onto the sidewalk. "How did you feel when you looked down on that dead body and saw it was somebody you knew? Huh? How did you feel looking down on somebody you loved, Detective Riley? Did you feel hurt? Huh? Did you feel helpless? Well that's exactly how I felt when I came to you and told you your nephew raped me and you did nothin'!"

My mouth almost dropped to the floor when I heard those words come out Frenchy's mouth. It explained a lot. It explained her anger. It explained her pain. It explained her resentment towards males and her willingness to stand up for herself and protect her family. Detective Riley stared at Frenchy and she stared back. Looking at Tammy and Glow's expression, I could tell that they were not surprised by Frenchy's announcement. Detective Riley's facial expression changed from anger to pity. I think he found the answers to the questions he was seeking, and probably a few more than he anticipated.

"You ladies have a good day," Detective Riley turned around and walked away.

As Detective Riley was walking away, Frenchy turned around and walked into the house. When she opened the door, I ran to her and wrapped my arms around her waist. She pulled me away from her and held up my face.

"You, OK?" Frenchy asked.

She was waiting for me to nod my head, for after all, I hadn't spoken a word since shortly after I was raped. But instead of nodding my head, for the first time in three weeks, I spoke.

"Are you OK, Frenchy?" I replied.

"Oh my God! You talked!" Frenchy yelled outside to Tammy and Glow. "Hey y'all! C'mere! Khloe talked!"

Tammy and Glow burst through the screen with excitement. They surrounded me and jumped up and down.

"Girl, say something else!" Glow shouted.

"What?" I laughed out loud.

"Say anything!" Tammy shouted.

"Wait! Wait! Wait!" Frenchy said. "Y'all stop yelling before you scare her to death!"

"OK! OK! OK!" Glow said. "I'm so glad we have you back!"

My three cousins hugged me for what seemed like a lifetime. It's funny, we never mentioned Money, or me being raped for the remainder of my time there in Memphis. It would be a few years before I would visit my family again. Despite that horrible traumatic experience, I finally felt what it was like to be a part of a loving family.

—

"How did your family in Bermuda react to your rape?" Dr. Turner asked.

"I thought that when I went back home to St. George, I would get sympathy and things would improve for me as far as stability. I was foolish and sadly mistaken to believe that I would receive love and affection from my family for the tragedy I had suffered. I was placed in the care of my mother, and the very first day I was home she began to antagonize me. You see, that wasn't the first time something like that had happened to me."

"Really?" Dr. Turner looked with serious concern. "What else happened to you, Khloe?"

Khloe did not respond initially. She was not prepared to go that far into her my past after revealing her rape in Memphis. Dr. Turner picked up on her reluctance and she backed off.

"Listen, Khloe," Dr. Turner said, trying to comfort her. "It's OK to take a little time. You've made great progress today. You should feel good about yourself."

"After almost ten years, I suppose it's time for some form of progress, Dr. Turner," Khloe replied. "Wow. Thank you."

"Don't thank me," Dr. Turner smiled. "I am just a listening ear. You are the one with the courage to confront your past and admit it out loud."

"I, uh," Khloe paused, "I would like to discuss more of my past, if you don't mind. That's if we have time."

"We have plenty of time. Please share," Dr. Turner nodded and smiled.

Khloe was beginning to feel more and more comfortable expressing her past to Dr. Turner. She felt that if she was able to make one breakthrough, then she may have been able to release some of her other internal demons as well. She had gone from apprehensive to eagerly excited to share her story, because she now had a willing platform, a platform that may not always be available to her. She was also concerned that if she stopped talking on that afternoon, that she may have never been able to muster the courage again.

"Please feel free to continue whenever you are ready, Khloe?" Dr. Turner asked.

"OK," Khloe answered. "I'm just taking a minute to get myself together."

"Again, take your time," Dr. Turner said.

"Whoo," Khloe took a very deep breath and then released.

Dr. Turner decided to give Khloe a moment alone to compose herself, while she came into the reception area to check on me. "I'm going to go make sure dad is alright out there. He's not used to being on that side of my door."

"OK," Khloe took another deep breath.

"Be right back."

"OK," Khloe smiled.

Dr. Turner walked out of her office and into the reception area where I was nervously waiting.

"So how are you doing out here on this side of the wall for a change, Mr. Simms?" Dr. Turner asked.

"It's a little different," I joked. "How are things going on in there?"

"She's doing very well, actually."

"She hasn't said anything about me, has she?" I asked.

"No, not yet," Dr. Turner chuckled.

"Good," I sighed. "Has she told you anything that she hasn't told me."

"Now you know how this goes, Mr. Simms. You're going to have to ask her that yourself," Dr. Turner smiled. "Doctor-patient confidentiality, remember?"

"Technically speaking, she's not really your patient. She's more of a stand-in," I joked.

"Stand-in, substitute, scab, the rules are the rules."

"I tried it."

"Yes sir, you did, nevertheless," Dr. Turner turned to re-enter her office. "I was just coming out to check on you. I'll go back in now and finish my discussion with Ms. Khloe."

"Speak highly of me," I advised. "Both of you."

"I'll talk to you later, Mr. Simms."

Dr. Turner walked into her office to finish her session with Khloe.

"Before I left, you had mentioned that your experience in Memphis was not the first time something like that had happened to you. Would you like to discuss what happened?"

"I, uh...well."

Without warning, Khloe's mood instantly changed. She looked at Dr. Turner with complete sadness, and Dr. Turner looked at Khloe with complete confusion. Dr. Turner put her notepad away and removed her eyeglasses from her face. She cleared her throat and spoke hoarsely.

"Is there something you want to say, Khloe?"

"Yes."

"Go ahead," Dr. Turner said with encouragement.

"I...I...," Khloe lowered her head and looked at the floor.

"Take your time."

"OK," Khloe paused again and then prepared to speak, but couldn't. She looked at Dr. Turner and then lowered her head and looked at the floor once again.

"It's OK, Khloe, it's OK."

Khloe raised her head and she began to speak candidly, for the first time, about the sexual molestation that she endured...

—

My mother and her sisters were adopted by Lily and Tyrone Carter. The Carters were my mother's maternal aunt and uncle. My Aunt Lily was my grandmother's sister. My grandmother died at an early age and my grandfather was never in the picture. My mother and my Uncle Craig, my Aunt Lily's son, were the same age and were raised as brother and sister. Which is why I identified him as my uncle and not my cousin. His full name was Craig Carter, and he was quite a shady character. My Aunt Lily always tried to protect him, even when she knew it was wrong. He stayed in and out of jail, even when he was a teen. But he could do nothing wrong in her eyes.

Growing up in school, it was kind of difficult for my mother to explain to people how two siblings, who were not twins, were in the same classes. As a matter of fact, they showed no family resemblance. My uncle and the rest of the Carter family were very light-skinned people, whereas my mother was very dark-skinned. Nevertheless, to the world, they pretended as if they were an immediate biological family of parents and siblings. From the outside looking in, no one would have known that my mother was adopted. However, the family bond was a façade that only existed to dupe the public because when my mother was home, she was a helpless victim of incest at the hands of my Uncle Craig and his brother, my Uncle Zachary, whom I was forced to call Uncle Zach.

Uncle Zach and Uncle Craig were the Carter's only two sons, and my mom was the only girl. My mother told me that at night they would sneak into her bedroom and commit sexual acts on her. Sometimes they would go alone, and sometimes they would go together. She said it started at a very early age and continued until she moved out of that house. She was afraid to tell anyone because she thought that no one would believe her. After all, she was the adopted child, so who would dare corroborate her story?

My mother told me that she would hide in her closet at night hoping her brothers would not find her. But they always did. There was literally no place for her to hide in that little three-bedroom home. My grandparents had a bedroom on one side of the house, and my mother's bedroom was directly across the hall from Uncle Craig and Uncle Zach, who shared a room.

My mother told me that one night both of my uncles came into her room. One laid on one side of her bed, and the other one laid on the other side. She said she laid on her stomach so that they couldn't touch between her legs. She tried to act like she was sleep but they kept handling her pretty rough, until she could no longer pretend.

"Stop!" Mom said.

"Be quiet," Uncle Zach whispered, "Mama and Daddy are going to hear you."

"Then leave me alone!" Mom said before Uncle Craig covered her mouth.

"Look, we ain't gon' do nothing to you. We just came in here to mess around. Stop acting so crazy."

"I want y'all to get out of here and leave me alone," Mom pleaded.

"Why you trippin', Clarice?" Uncle Craig asked. "You ain't never said nothing before."

"Because I don't feel like doing nothing with y'all tonight. I'm tired and I want to get some sleep, so leave me alone."

"OK," Uncle Zach said, "how about if one of us leave and the other one stay?"

"No! I want both of y'all to leave! Now!" Mom yelled.

"Be quiet, Clarice," Uncle Zach whispered. "If you wake mama and daddy up, all of us are going to be in trouble."

"I don't care! Get outta' here!"

"Listen," Uncle Zach said, "Craig is gettin' ready to leave."

"No, I ain't, you leave, Zach."

"I don't care who leave, just get the hell out!" Mom tried to climb over Uncle Craig, and he grabbed her by the waist and pulled her on top of him. "Let me go, Craig! I ain't playing with you!"

"We just wanna' touch you," Uncle Craig said, as he accidentally ripped my mother's gown. "See what you made me do?"

"You know we ain't gon' do nothin' to you, girl!" Uncle Zach snarled under his breath.

"STOOOOOOOOOOOOOOOOOP!" Mom screamed.

A few minutes later the light came on and my grandfather stood in the doorway and saw my mother, Uncle Zach and Uncle Craig lying in the bed together. He stared at them and shook his head. Unbelievably, he cut off the light and turned around and walked away. At that moment, my mother's heart and her spirit were broken. She laid on her back and let my uncles have their way. She told me that was the last night she spent in that house. She ran away and eventually joined the United States Army.

—

"I'm a little confused," Dr. Turner said. "You began referring to yourself as being molested, but you told the story of your mother being the one who was actually molested. So, which of you was actually molested? You or your mother?"

"Both of us. By the same man," Khloe said.

Khloe looked down at the floor and shook her head.

"By your uncle?" Dr. Turner said angrily.

"Yes, Dr. Turner," I mumbled and looked down at the floor.

"Khloe!" Dr. Turner held my face in her hands, "It's OK. It's OK, you can talk to me. What the hell happened?"

Dr. Turner was the consummate professional. She had toed the line of professionalism with Khloe throughout their session. She knew that she was crossing the line by allowing her feelings to personalize Khloe's experience. At that point, I believe that she made a conscientious decision to choose compassion over professionalism.

"I'm not so sure that I want to talk about this right now, Dr. Turner. I thought I was ready but thinking about all of this is making me feel some kind of way," Khloe said.

"You don't have to talk about anything that makes you feel uncomfortable. If you would like to share your feelings, you don't have to refer to anyone by name. I want what you want. I want you to heal from what happened to you."

Khloe lowered her head and stared at the floor. She started to become fidgety with her hands as she struggled to speak the words that were trying to escape her mouth.

"Breathe, and take your time," Dr. Turner said.

"Whoo," Khloe sighed, "OK..."

—

When...when I was six years old my mother made me go live with my adoptive grandparents, the Carters. That was the first time it happened to me...on my sixth birthday. My Uncle Craig stopped by to give me a lollipop. My mother was gone, and my grandparents weren't really paying close attention to us, when my uncle took me by the hand and led me into my mother's old bedroom. He sat on the bed and then he sat me on his lap. He handed me the lollipop and kissed my forehead.

"How's my pretty little girl?" Uncle Craig kissed me on my cheek and then helped me unwrap the lollipop.

"Good," I said, anxious to taste my lollipop.

Uncle Craig picked me up and repositioned me on his lap. He sat me down on his fully erect penis. Although I could feel his hard penis beneath me, at that young age, I was still unaware of what was actually going on. I saw it as strange, but not necessarily sexual.

"You look pretty in your birthday dress, little girl," Uncle Craig said.

"Thank you, Uncle Craig," I said as I began to lick my lollipop.

"Do you like the way that sucker taste?"

"Yeah," I said.

"Can Uncle Craig have a lick?"

I held out my sucker for Uncle Craig to lick. He stuck the lollipop into his mouth and then back into mine. He did it twice more and then held it in his mouth.

"You want to lick it at the same time?" Uncle Craig asked.

I hunched my shoulders because I did not totally comprehend what he meant. Uncle Craig and I licked the lollipop at the same time. He twirled his tongue around the lollipop until his tongue was touching mine.

"Your tongue taste sweet. Can Uncle Craig taste it again?"

I didn't say anything because it felt too strange. My uncle removed the lollipop altogether and he continued to slide his tongue inside of my mouth. He started to rub my legs up and then down all the way from my thighs to my ankles.

"You are such a pretty little girl, Khloe," Uncle Craig said, "Yes, yes, yes, you are such a pretty little girl; so, so, pretty. You like the way I rub your leg?"

"Yes," I said. I really didn't feel one way or the other. It was just a hand on my leg.

Uncle Craig started to breathe harder as his hands went higher and higher towards my panties. He finally moved my panties to the side and said, "Uncle Craig is not going to hurt you, OK? I'm just going to make you feel good for your birthday."

I didn't say anything. I just remember feeling piercing pain as he slid one finger, and then two, inside of me. I started to cry and he rocked me on his knee.

"Shh! It's OK. Don't that feel good?" Uncle Craig asked.

"No," I cried, "it hurts."

"Shh!" Uncle Craig covered my mouth. "It will start feeling good in a minute. It's your birthday and Uncle Craig is going to make you feel really good, alright?'

"Alright," I said reluctantly.

"Oh yeah," Uncle Craig closed his eyes and started to moan.

When Uncle Craig heard people walking down the hall towards the bedroom, he quickly removed his hand from my panties and pushed me off of his lap.

"Shh!" Uncle Craig whispered. "Don't tell nobody Uncle Craig rubbed your leg because you will get in big trouble, OK?"

"OK," I said.

My mother walked through the door holding my younger sister in her arms. My mother burst through the door with a huge smile on her face until she saw me sitting next to Uncle Craig.

"Where's my bir...?" Mom stopped in her tracks. "What the hell are you doing with my daughter, Craig?"

"What you mean?" Uncle Craig asked nervously.

"You know what I mean. Why y'all back here all by yourself?" Mom grabbed my hand and snatched me off of the bed and screamed at me. "Who told you to come back here?"

When my mother started to yell at me it scared me. She scared me more than Uncle Craig at that point, and I didn't know what to say.

"She came back here on her own. What you want me to do?"

"Get out of here, Khloe!" Mom snapped.

I thought my mother was angry with me because I had let Uncle Craig touch me. In my young mind, Uncle Craig had told the truth. It seemed to me that my mother wasn't angry with him, she was angry with me. I looked back at Uncle Craig as my mother was pulling me out of the room, and he placed his fingers over his lips gesturing for me to be silent.

My mother went against her husband to spend my birthday with me, but the next week she pulled another disappearing act. One afternoon when I was supposed to be picked up from school, my grandparents weren't feeling well, so my Uncle Craig volunteered. I was sitting in my classroom with my teacher when he walked in. I was surprised and afraid at the same time. I wasn't afraid of him as I would fear a monster, I was afraid that he would make me feel uncomfortable as he did before, and I did not want to feel that way. I loved him as my uncle, but the truth was…he was a monster!

He explained to my teacher that he was my uncle and had come to pick me up. I looked at my teacher for help because I did not want to go with him. I did not want him to make me feel good, as he falsely promised before, and have my mother become angry with me again.

"Come on, pretty girl," Uncle Craig said, "time to go home."

"See you tomorrow," my teacher waved goodbye to me.

I looked back at my teacher, as my uncle took my hand and led me out of the school. He held my hand in his and we walked down the street. My grandparents didn't live far from the school, so I was familiar with the route. I was so familiar with the route, that I noticed when we passed my grandparents' house and continued to walk.

"Where are we going, Uncle Craig?" I asked.

"We're going to get some candy from the store, pretty girl," Uncle Craig smiled and rubbed his hand up and down my back as we walked along the street. "You want some candy?"

"Yes," I said excitedly.

We stopped in the store and Uncle Craig bought me a few pieces of candy. When we left the store, we went directly to Uncle Craig's house. He turned on the TV and asked me if I wanted to watch cartoons. I told him that I did, and I sat on the floor with my legs folded eating my candy. My uncle disappeared for a moment and then he returned and laid behind me. He slowly started to rub my back.

"You know you're a very pretty girl, don't you, Khloe?"

"Thank you, Uncle Craig."

"You're even prettier than some of the grown ladies I know."

Uncle Craig kissed me on the forehead, then my cheek, and then my lips. He pulled me backwards until my head was lying on his stomach.

"Hold on a second, pretty girl. I'll be right back."

My uncle went into his bedroom and then returned wearing an old robe and some white tube socks. He laid on the floor next to me and untied his robe. He had taken off all of his clothes and was now completely naked on the floor with me.

"Have you ever seen one of these before?" Uncle Craig said, as he held his penis in his hand and continued to rub my back.

I lowered my head and looked toward the floor. Uncle Craig lifted my head and made me look at him.

"You want to touch it?" Uncle Craig asked.

I did not respond. My uncle took my hand and placed it on his penis. He covered my hand with his and started a slow, up and down stroking motion. He closed his eyes and laid back, continuing to move my hand up and down. Uncle Craig began to moan louder and louder until he reached his orgasm. His semen leaked all over my hand, and once again he was able to convert from perverted predator to loving uncle.

"I'm so sorry, babygirl," Uncle Craig said. "Don't move. Let me get you a towel."

Uncle Craig went to the bathroom and returned with a towel with which he gently wiped my hands dry.

"Now once again, Khloe, you can't tell anyone because everyone will be mad at you, OK?"

165

I nodded my head.

"OK, you wanna' go to grandma and grandpa house?"

I nodded my head again.

"You want your last piece of candy to eat on the way?"

Once again, I nodded.

"Let's go," Uncle Craig took me by the hand and took me to my grandparent's house as if nothing had happened.

I never forgot that day. When I grew older, I promised myself that if I ever saw him again, I would kill him on sight. Six years later and there I was again, in Memphis, Tennessee, once again being sexually assaulted.

My aunts told my mother what happened. You would think that she would have compassion for me. But she didn't. She was angry with me. I recall the conversation I had with her when I returned from Memphis.

"Everywhere you go trouble seem to follow, especially when it comes to boys. You need to sit your fast ass down somewhere and stop chasin' up behind these boys all of the time. I don't know where you got that from anyway. Ain't nan' one of us in this family hot like you. I don't know how you turned out like that, but you sho' didn't get that from me."

"Ma, I'm not a fast girl."

"How come this only happen to you? Why not your cousins?"

"Mama?" I cried, "I don't know. I didn't do nothin'. What kind of girl do you think I am?"

"A fast one!"

"I'm not fast! I can't help it if these grown men keep trying to mess with me. I don't want them to. I want them to leave me alone."

My mother stared at me with an evil look and said, "You think I don't know about you and Craig?"

"Know what?"

"I know what y'all used to do."

"We ain't do nothing, Ma."

"Oh yes you did!"

"I promise. I don't know what you are talking about, Ma."

"Tell me the truth!" Mom shouted. "You let that man touch you, didn't you?"

"No ma'am!" I shouted back with tears in my eyes.

"I said tell me the truth!"

"OK! OK!" I shouted. "He touched me. But I didn't want him to!"

"You tramp!" Mom said.

"Tramp?" I was angry. "You calling me a tramp, Ma? What are you?"

"You better watch your mouth!" Mom said.

"Mama, I'm only twelve years old! Where was you when Uncle Craig put his hands on me? Huh? Where was you when that boy raped me?"

"I had to take care of myself! My husband! And my family!"

"Everybody but me, huh, Ma? I wasn't a part of that family?"

I could immediately tell that I went too far. I had never stood up to my mother before. I was always her protector and supporter.

"I don't have to stand here and listen to this 'cause you gon' make me hurt you!" Mom walked out of the house and slammed the door.

Our relationship was never the same. Well, not until we talked, and she confessed to me why she was so angry at me in that kitchen. It was not me that she truly felt contempt and anger, it was herself. She felt that I was molested because she did not stop her brothers when they sexually assaulted her.

—

"That day had a lasting impression on me. It began my descent into a lonely and introversive place," Khloe said.

"Did you feel as if you had nowhere to turn?" Dr. Turner asked.

"I was still too young and too confused as to what was happening to me, as far as incestuous molestation, so I didn't feel a need to have to turn to anyone. My mother's personality was always erratic, so I didn't relate my uncle touching me to my mother's outburst. I related my mother's outburst to her erratic behavior. But in hindsight, I think I gained a greater understanding of what happened, and what happens in families when it comes to sexual assault."

"And what is that?" Dr. Turner asked.

"As a society, this happens a lot more than what we are willing to admit. And when we keep it shut in like I have, it doesn't have a safe place to release the pain and shame. But I feel better having told you. I feel much, much, much better."

"That's wonderful, Khloe," Dr. Turner smiled. "Do you ever plan on telling your father what happened to you?"

"Someday."

"You don't think this is something he should know or would want to know?"

"You don't know my dad. He hasn't always been this mild-mannered, and if I tell him, there's no telling what he would do."

"I understand," Dr. Turner nodded. "But I want you to put yourself in his shoes for a moment and think about if it was your child who was sexually assaulted. Would you want to know?"

"I'm sure I would. But if I had the benefit of knowing that I was once the person my father once was, I think it would be better if I did not know."

"And that's perfectly fine," Dr. Turner smiled.

"I cannot thank you enough for this afternoon, Dr. Turner. You gave me in a one-hour session what my other therapists failed to accomplish over years of therapy."

"Thank you very much for the kind words, but today was about you. You were simply ready to take on your past today, and I was here for support."

"Thank you just the same."

"Hold on, please," Dr. Turner opened her door to call me into her office. "Mr. Simms? We're ready for you."

I walked into Dr. Turner's office, and I could see that Khloe had been crying. The tracks of her tears streamed down her face. But the smile she was wearing was bright and full of happiness.

"Hey," I said to Khloe.

"Hi, Daddy," Khloe smiled.

"Ready to go?" I asked.

"Yup," Khloe said. "Goodbye, Dr. Turner. Thank you. Thank you so much."

"Good luck, Khloe."

"I guess I'll be seeing you next week then, Doc," I said.

"Yes, sir. See you next week."

CHAPTER EIGHT

The year of 2020...

When I returned for my next session; I had a little surprise for Dr. Turner. It was an unexpected surprise.

"Good afternoon, Mr. Simms. How's Khloe?" Dr. Turner asked.

"She's doing fantastic. I've never seen her so happy and excited about life. Whatever you told her, it worked."

"It wasn't so much what I told her, but what she told me. Sometimes it takes a stranger to tell us our problems to make things a lot easier."

"Whatever your method is, keep doing it."

"So, how do you feel about Khloe's session, Mr. Simms?"

"I…I am happy. I am happy because she's happy. I just wish that I knew what you all discussed that made her so happy."

"Need I remind you, Mr. Simms?"

"I know. I know. Doctor-patient confidentiality."

"Good."

"I have a very small, miniscule request."

"I'm listening," Dr. Turner said.

"Being that we had so much success with Khloe, I decided to bring my daughter, Kiera. Is that going to bring a problem?"

"No," Dr. Turner chuckled. "That won't be a problem at all."

"Great, without further ado, I'd like for you to meet my middle child, Kiera," as I spoke, I opened the door and gestured for Kiera to enter Dr. Turner's office.

Dr. Turner stood and shook my daughter Kiera's hand, "Good afternoon, Kiera. How are you, today?"

"I'm fine."

"Well honey, I'm going to let you talk to Dr. Turner for a while. I won't be far away. I'll be right out here, OK?"

"OK, dad," Kiera said.

I walked into the reception area and grabbed a magazine. I felt much more comfortable with Kiera than I felt with Khloe being in that office.

"Well, Kiera, please feel free to say whatever you want to say. This is a safe space for you to express yourself on things that you are comfortable saying, and things that you may not be so comfortable expressing. I'm not here to judge. I'm only here to listen."

"OK, can I start?" Kiera asked.

"Um, uh…sure," Dr. Turner was surprised at how quickly Kiera was willing to share her issues.

"So, where do you want me to start?" Kiera asked.

"Let's start from the beginning,"

"The beginning of what? My life?"

"Wherever you feel comfortable starting," Dr. Turner suggested.

"Alright...," Kiera said. "I guess my life started out like shit. Oh, excuse me, can I cuss in here?"

"Speak however you want to speak. I am here to listen to you with the best way that you can communicate."

"Good. Cause I cuss all the dam time. I just can't control that shit. But don't get it twisted, I can give you the bathroom or the boardroom. I'm just sayin'.

"Fine," Dr. Turner nodded.

"Anyways, when I was born, my mother didn't know who my father was because she was having sex with three different men at the same time. On three different occasions, she went to all three of the men and told them that they were the father. It was strange, because neither of them played a major role in my life, but then all of them played enough of a small role in my upbringing that I thought having three dads was normal. Mom had trained me how to keep my mouth shut about the other dads and encouraged me to just accept whatever time I had with either one of them. Neither of them knew about the other, until one day all three showed up at her apartment at the same time and started talking. It turned out that my mother was getting child support from all three. That's when they decided to have a paternity test to prove who was my actual father. When all of the tests came back, guess what? Andre Simms, you are the father! The other two potential dads offered my dad their condolences and got the hell out of my life...forever.

"I was born on December 31st, 1993 in Los Angeles, California. My mother, Cheryl Cambridge, was an addict and she often suffered from delusions. Being a child, I suffered the repercussions from her disease, and the pain continued throughout my entire days as a youth. Don't get me wrong, I

174

loved my mother more than life itself, but I had to grow up fast because there were times when she would check out of reality and I had to step up. Other than child support, there was only so much my father could do, because he lived way over here on the east coast. He would encourage me to be strong and to take care of my mother, because he understood how I felt since he went through a similar situation with his mother.

"My dad was my rock. Once my father and I became comfortable with our father-daughter relationship, we developed a very special bond. He and I would talk on the phone sometimes from the early evening until three of four o'clock in the morning. My mother would sometime get jealous because of our relationship, but she would never interfere. I never asked my dad for anything other than his love. His love and attention were very important for me, in order for me to love myself. He would come visit me every summer, and I would cry happy tears when he arrived, and sad tears when he left. He was everything to me.

"He would pick me up from my mother's house, and we would go to a nice, elegant hotel for a week. He tried to make up for the time he was away by doing everything under the sun. We would make trips to McDonald's, Disneyland, Big Bear Mountain, and other attractions. As I became older, we would do more big girl things. I was artistically inclined, and I wanted to go to concerts and museums. I don't think my dad was into all of that, but he never said a word. Whatever I wanted to do… we did.

"In my early teens, my dad started to notice that I dressed more like a tomboy than a young lady, so he started to ask me about boys. I would ignore him and try to change the subject. My dad wasn't a fool. He noticed that I was noticing girls much more than boys. Finally, he asked me if I liked girls. I told him that if he wasn't ready for the truth, then he may want to retract his question. He said my sexual orientation didn't matter to him, and that he would love me no matter who I loved. That's when he became my hero. I felt like I could open up and tell him anything. He became my protector and my encourager. I wasn't foolish enough to believe that he wanted me to be a lesbian, but I was very confident that he wanted me to be happy, and boys did not make me happy in the romance department. I started to visit him in Atlanta after that. That's when my eyes were opened to the wonderful and rainbow world of lesbianism.

"My relationship with my mother was complex. We both played the roles of mother and child. I was the oldest child of three. I often took care of my mother and my siblings. I had to make sure that my siblings ate, were dressed and ready for school. After we were taken from my mother a few times, I knew that I had to make sure that our family stayed together. When my mother was not high, she was loving and gentle. She was the best mother a child could want. But when she was high, she was mean, ornery, and delusional. It became too much, just too much."

"You seemed to have taken on a huge responsibility for a child. But you seemed to have managed. What happened that was too much?"

"Well..."

—

The older I became, the more responsibilities I was given. The more responsibilities I was given, the more my mother drifted into the world of drug abuse. When I turned thirteen, my responsibilities increased drastically, and I was almost solely responsible for the welfare of my siblings and myself.

"You know those people are going to come take y'all away from me 'cause you went down there runnin' your mouth, don't you?" Mom asked.

"What did I do?" I asked.

"You told them folks that you ain't had nothin' to eat."

"That's not what happened, Mommy. They asked me to tell them the last time I ate, and I told them."

"Well, they sent me a letter and they said that they are going to take you and your little brother and sister away from me. Are you happy? Is that what you wanted?"

"They're not going to take us anywhere."

"Who's gonna' stop them?"

"Mommy?" I said, "All that we have to do is tell 'em that I lied. They ain't takin' us nowhere."

"It's too late now. You shoulda' thought about lyin' when they asked you in the first place. I don't know what we gon' do now. Maybe it's best y'all go with them until I get my shit together anyway."

"Don't talk like that, Mommy. It's always gon' be us. You, me, Leonard and Morgan. And it's gon' always be us."

"I need to get outta' here. They gon' come here and take y'all away from me and put me in jail. I can't go back to jail. Uh-uhn. I can't go."

"Mommy listen to me. No one is coming to take us away from you. I need you to just go take a nap, and when you wake up everything will be alright."

"Ah, I know what's going on. You want them to take me to jail, don't you? You want me outta' the way so you can take over my house. Well, that ain't gon' happen."

"Mommy listen to yourself. You need a nap...please."

"Naw, I'm not going to sleep. You tryin' to get them people after me."

"Mommy! Nobody is coming to get you, OK? Nobody is coming to get you, and nobody is coming to get us."

"I hear 'em. I hear 'em coming. I gotta' get outta' here."

My mother ran towards the door and tried to open it. I slammed the door shut and tried to stop her from leaving.

"Let me outta' here!" Mom shouted.

My mother was on a really bad trip, and she didn't appear to be coming down anytime soon. I didn't want to let her out, because she was not in her right mind. When she was like that, she would leave and be gone for days. As tough as I had to be, I could not stand to see my mother walk out of that door. Despite my begging and pleading for her to stay, I was not stronger than the influence of the drug that possessed her.

"Mommy, please," I cried with tears in my eyes.

"MOVE!" Mom screamed.

"NO!" I screamed back.

My mother reached for a knife and snatched my head backwards by my ponytail. She held the knife to my throat and snarled, "Get outta' my way or I will cut your throat from ear to ear. Do you hear me?"

"Yes, ma'am," I said as I released my grip on the doorknob.

My mother opened the door and walked out on us. I knew that it wasn't my mother who was walking out, it was the person possessed by the drugs, but it hurt just as bad. I sat on the floor in the middle of the kitchen and cried.

My mother didn't return until the next morning. She came and picked up my sister Morgan, who was three years old, and headed right back out for my sister's doctor's appointment. I waited and waited until late in the afternoon, but she never came back. Around six o'clock that evening our phone rang, and it was the clinic asking for my mom. They said Morgan had been at the clinic since that morning when my mother had dropped her off. I fed my little brother Leonard, who was nine. I dressed him as quickly as I could, and we left the house headed for the clinic. By the time I arrived at the clinic, they were closing their office. There I was, a child myself, coming to pick up a toddler.

"Hi, I'm here to pick up my little sister, Morgan," I said.

"Where's your mother?" the receptionist asked.

"I don't know."

"Where's your dad?"

"I don't know."

"Do you have any grandparents?"

"They're dead."

"I'm sorry, but we can't release this child to you, you're too young."

"I know I'm young, but I take care of my sister and my brother all of the time."

"You take care of your sister and brother all of the time?"

"Yeah," I said, "sometime when my mother is not feeling

good.""What is your name?" the receptionist asked.

"Kiera."

"Will there be an adult at home waiting for you?"

"Yes, ma'am. My mother should be back from the store by the time we get home," I said. "Can I have my sister now, please ma'am?"

"I thought you said you didn't know where your mother was?"

"Oh, she's at the store. She told me to come pick up my sister while she gets us something to eat tonight."

"You don't have any food at home?"

"Yes...uh, no," I said nervously.

"Could you hold on a second?" the receptionist walked to the back of the office and left me at the desk.

Something told me to just take off, but I couldn't abandon my sister. I stood at the desk and waited for the receptionist to bring Morgan to me. Out of nowhere, I saw the flashing police blue and red police lights pull in front of the door. A police officer got out and entered the building. The receptionist went over to him and started whispering. The police looked over the receptionist's shoulder and looked at me. He then started to walk toward me. I knew the jig was up.

"How are you doing today, little lady?" the police officer asked.

"I'm fine," I said.

"Where's your mother or your dad?"

"I don't know," I said.

"Well, who's taking care of you?"

"I am," I said.

"Don't you think you're too young to take care of yourself?"

"No, officer. I'm a teenager."

"Well, I'm going to see if I can fix it so that you don't have to worry about taking care of your little brother and sister."

Fix it my ass. It was on that day that they tore my family apart, and I would have to fight like hell to see my siblings again. They placed all three of us in different homes. My mother was nowhere to be found. I was shipped from home to home until I ended up with the Blakes. The Blakes were an affluent middle-aged, white couple who were unable to have children. Although they were British and living in Malibu temporarily, it was still a long way from Compton where I was born and raised.

The Blakes were Catholic. I was raised in a Baptist church. There was a stark difference in the way the two services were conducted. In the Catholic church there was the reading of scriptures, a few prayers, and then we got the hell out of there. Boring but quick. In the Baptist church, there would be an offering, the choir would sing, another offering, followed by another offering, leading to another song by the choir, finishing up with tithing. Then, there would be a warm-up sermon to get the church hyped before the pastor came on as the main event.

The Blakes were good people who had very pure and positive intent. They did not want a dime for caring after me. They only wanted to share their humanity and prosperity with someone who needed it. The only problem-- they didn't know shit about black people. They didn't know what to do with my hair. They didn't know what type of music I listened to, although I will admit that they turned me on to a lot of shit I had never heard before. They didn't know what type of clothes I liked. I was born in a hip-hop culture, but they wanted me to wear a lot of corny Ivy League shit. They didn't know the type of food that I liked. Eating all that bland food was killing my ass. They said it was healthier. Shiiiiiiit, I was like, let me die then. They were patient people, and they understood that I was entering a totally new culture, so they took the time to learn about me and the black culture.

Overall, I came to love the Blakes. Unfortunately, they were only going to be in the country for a year and then go back to England. They were philanthropists and humanitarians who truly wanted to make a difference in the world. Fortunately for me, I was at the wrong place at the right time. They fell in love with me at first sight, and the rest is history.

A few months after I arrived, the Blakes were approved to foster another young lady named April. April was two years older than me. I thought I had problems, until I met April. April was grossly obese, and she had a lot of other medical problems that were inherited at birth. But she was also born with a heart of gold. I didn't see it at first, but it didn't take long for me to find out. She had a beautiful soul.

When the Blakes brought her home, I could not help but stare and feel sorry for her. She had trouble breathing and moving around. Just taking a few steps would sometimes overwhelm her, and she would have to stop and catch her breath. I tried to avoid talking to her or spending time with her. I thought that just because we were in the same house, it didn't mean that we had to act like we were real sisters. I felt sorry for her, until she and I finally had a chance to talk one-on-one. The day after she arrived, she and I were the only two at home and she was getting food out of the refrigerator. I walked in the kitchen and I stopped in my tracks and I just stared at her. She finally noticed me standing there, and then she started to stare back at me as I was staring at her.

"What?" April asked as she was opening her mouth to put food in it.

"Huh?" I was caught off guard.

"Why are you staring at me?" April asked.

"I wasn't staring. I was just looking."

"What's the difference?"

"I mean, you're in the kitchen so it's kind of hard for me to miss you."

"Really? Is that supposed to be a joke about my weight?" April asked.

"No. What does your weight have to do with anything?"

"'I mean, you're in the kitchen so it's kind of hard for me to miss you,' isn't that what you just said?" April repeated, mocking Kiera.

"Yeah, that's what I said but who said I was saying that because of your weight? I woulda' said that about anybody."

"Really?"

"Yeah."

"OK, girl. Whatever."

"No, don't whatever me. I wasn't talking about your weight. I mean, it's just you and me in here, so of course I'm gon' see you."

"OK, if you say so, it's just, whatever," April hunched her shoulders.

"Why you keep sayin' that?" I became frustrated because it seemed that April was trying to force me to admit to something that I was not trying to do.

183

"It's no big deal. I'm overweight. I'mma big girl. I know it. It's cool. I know people stare at me and talk about me. I'm used to it."

"But don't that hurt your feelings?" I asked.

"It used to, but now I'm like, whatever man."

"I wish I was like you."

"Really?"

"Because I'm not like most girls, and when people find out my little secret it's like they call me names and I can't stand that shit. I'm still the same person. It's just that I like…well, that's irrelevant. I'm still the same person."

"Go on and say it, you like girls. Ain't nothin' wrong with that."

"How did you know?" I asked.

"It doesn't take a rocket scientist to figure out that you're not into boys. If that's your preference, then hey, do you."

"Do you think the Blakes know I like girls?"

"Uh, a-hell no. Those people don't have a clue about anything other than Malibu and saving the world from all of its problems."

"They're good people, though," I said. "I'm glad to have them as foster parents."

"They're the best. I don't think my mother knows who my father was. She was an addict and didn't want me, so I kept ending up back in the system being rejected and neglected because nobody else wanted me either."

"Wow, I went through the same with my mother. She was hooked, too, and I had to take care of my little brother and sister until the children's services called the cops on my ass. They split us up and I don't know where they are."

"Dam, at least it was just me. So how do you cope with not being able to see your kid brother and sister?"

"That shit is hard. As much as I used to hate having to take care of them all the time, I miss them so much. I've been trying to reach my daddy so he can come get me."

"You got a daddy?"

"Yeah, everybody got a daddy. They may not be there, but they exist."

"Right," April laughed. "You don't have your father's number?"

"It was in my mama's phone. I had it wrote down, too, but when they took us to child services I couldn't go home and get shit. So I don't know how to contact him. And he doesn't know where the hell I am," I said.

"Are you and your dad close?" April asked.

"Oh my God, yes," I exclaimed with excitement. "I love my daddy so much. He come out here just to see me and then I go see him in Atlanta."

"Where's your mom?"

"I don't know. When she on that shit she just leaves and then come back whenever she comes down. She probably been back to the house and found out that child's services done took us. She probably ain't even trying to find us."

As we were talking, the Blakes returned and they came into the kitchen. They had very serious looks of concern on their faces. They stood on one side of the island in the middle of the kitchen while April was seated on one side, and I was standing on the other. They looked at each other then and smiled. Then they looked at us and did not smile. I knew it was something serious.

"Girls," Mr. Blake said. "I think we have a problem. Nothing that can't be fixed, but it's a problem just the same."

"As Mr. Blake and I were getting packages out of the back seat of the car, we happened to notice this on the floor," Mrs. Blake held a joint in her hand and raised it in the air. "We are in tune with society and we know that marijuana is now a recreational pastime, or a medicinal treatment, but it should still be used properly and accordingly with or by adult supervision when it comes to minors."

"So, who does this belong to?" Mr. Blake took the joint out of Mrs. Blake's hand and laid it on the island countertop, as if it was the smoking gun to a major homicide.

April looked at me and I looked at her. The Blakes waited patiently for one of us to confess to being the culprit.

"I'm sorry, Mr. and Mrs. Blake. It's mine. I didn't realize it had fell out. I should have told you that I use it for medicinal purposes to help with my pain."

"Ohhhh," Mrs. Blake walked over to April and put her arms around her. "Oh, we didn't mean to come off harsh or insensitive. We didn't know, sweetheart."

"We owe you an apology, April. "We should not have come off as accusatory. We should have simply inquired as to why you were using, instead of trying to find out who was using."

"It was a matter of miscommunication, that's all. Thank you for caring enough to ask," April said.

I thought to myself, what the hell just happened up in here. How did she turn this around to have the Blakes apologizing to her for

having weed in their car? Later that night, I went to April's bedroom and knocked on her door.

"Come in," April answered.

I walked in and saw that April was wearing a mask and breathing through a machine. She was lying on her back in her bed.

"Whoa, what's that?" I asked.

"A machine to help me breathe at night when I sleep," April answered.

"Do you have to use this every night?"

"Yup, and sometimes during the day."

"I bet that sucks."

"It doesn't suck as much as being dead," April chuckled through her mask.

"I feel you."

April removed her mask and then sat up, "So, what's up?"

"Thank you for not snitching on me and for taking the hit for that joint," I said with sincere gratitude.

"Don't worry about it. That's what big sisters do."

"Big sisters? You wanna' be my big sister?"

"Look, we don't have a choice, we're in this together. Blood don't always make you family. Situations, circumstances and love do. We're sisters."

No one had ever simply wanted to be my family that didn't have to be, so I was like, dam. I mean, that was some heavy shit for me.

"Sisters, huh?"

"Yup," April said as she put her mask back on. "But for right now, can this sister get a little time to herself? I got a little somethin'-somethin' goin' on right now."

"OK, bet," I chuckled as I backed out of her room. Granted, I still wanted April to be healthy, but I was not feeling sorry for her anymore.

At the end of the summer when it was time for school to start, they placed us in a private school where we had to wear uniforms. They did not have sizes that fit April, so the Blakes had to have her uniforms custom made. I was embarrassed for her, but she seemed to take it in stride. The Blakes had a gift for making everyone feel special, no matter who they were, and they were successful in making April and me feel special. When we went to be fitted for our school uniforms, Mrs. Blake took us to her personal tailor. I went first and her tailor, Mrs. Winbush, measured me and gave me my size. When she began to measure April, she made an insulting joke about April's size and that was the first time I ever saw Mrs. Blake angry.

"OK, now what's your name?" Mrs. Winbush asked.

"My name is Kiera," I responded.

"Kiera? That sounds like a princess' name.

"Thank you," I replied.

I stood on a stool in front of a three-angled mirror while Mrs. Winbush took my measurements. She wrote them down and then handed them to Mrs. Blake.

"Well, honey, that's about all I need. You can step down now."

I stepped down, and then Mrs. Blake called for April to come have her measurements. April had walked with a cane off and on since she eleven years old because she had issues getting around. It was taking her a while to get to the back of the shop, so I went and helped her.

"WOW! It's going to take a lot of material to get that girl in a uniform that fits," Mrs. Winbush said.

I don't know if April heard her, and I never asked, but I certainly did. And I was pissed. But if you think I was pissed, you should have seen Mrs. Blake.

"What did you say?" Mrs. Blake asked.

"Don't worry about it, it was just a poor attempt at joking," Mrs. Winbush chuckled.

"A poor attempt at a joke?" Mrs. Blake snapped. "Uh, girls? Could you go wait in the car for me, I'll be right out."

April and I turned around and started to go get in the car, as Mrs. Blake suggested, but her fuse was already lit and she could not wait for us to get completely out of the shop before she exploded on Mrs. Winbush.

"How dare you?" Mrs. Blake growled.

"OK, it was a bad joke. I'm sorry."

"You're damn right you're sorry. You're a sorry excuse for a human being."

"It was just a joke, honey, calm down," Mrs. Winbush pleaded.

"I'll tell you a joke and I promise you, it is hilarious," Mrs. Winbush said sarcastically. "Every Saturday morning when you think your husband is out golfing with the guys? Well, he's not. He's at his country club showcasing his mistress to all of his buddies. Now, how about that for poor judgment?"

Mrs. Blake stormed out of the shop, slinging the door open as she marched towards the car. She was so angry that I don't think she realized that she had walked past April and me on her way to the car, until she opened her car door and realized that we weren't in the car yet. When we arrived at the car, she looked at us and we looked at her, and all three of us laughed.

"I hate you girls had to see me like that, but sometimes American white people just get on my dam nerves," Mrs. Blake joked.

—

The rest of the school year flew by, and we had a ball. Not only did I have a mother and father, but I also had a sister. As our year was coming to an end, we knew the Blakes were going to have to go back home to England, and that we were going to have to be placed somewhere else. That would mean that April and I were going to be separated as well. I wasn't really concerned about me. I was concerned about April and her health. However, I wanted to make sure that she would be in a loving environment where people would take care of her.

But no matter how sick April was, she always cared about other people more than herself. She went online, and after a thorough research, she was able to locate my father. She gave me the information, and that is how my father and I reconnected. He arranged to assume custody of me, and the Blakes planned a small intimate farewell party to be held on the day my father arrived to pick me up.

To say that I was uncontrollably excited would be a tremendous understatement. April and the Blakes were outside on the back patio enjoying their time together. I kept pacing back and forth to the front of the house, waiting for my father's car to pull up. The Blakes and April teased me about my excitement, but I was at a point where I was no longer able to contain it. When the headlights of my father's car finally turned into the driveway, I ran out to meet him.

"Daddy!" I screamed, as I jumped into my dad's arms.

"Ohhhhh! My baby girl! Daddy's been looking all over for you," Daddy said, as he spun me around.

It felt surreal as I walked my father through the house and onto the patio, where the Blakes and April were waiting. I introduced my dad, and we all had a good time. Dad thanked the Blakes for watching over me, and the Blakes thanked Dad for allowing them to share their time with me. It was certainly a kumbaya moment. But when the moment came for me to leave, the laughter and smiles became saddened tears. April and I wanted a moment alone, so she walked me to my room to help me with my luggage. As we were packing, I couldn't help but thank God for how much He had blessed me with. I came to the Blakes with nothing but the clothes on my back. I was leaving with three suitcases and two duffle bags.

"This is a whole lot of shit for somebody who came here with nothing," I joked.

"I'm saying," April joked back. "When did you have time to hoard all this stuff, girl?"

"I don't even know, but I got it! It's mine! And I'm keeping it!"

"Come here," April reached out her arms and she started to cry, and I ran into her arms. "You big baby, what are you crying for?"

"I'm gonna' miss you."

"I'm gonna' miss you, too. But it's OK, you're going to Atlanta with your dad."

"I wish you could come with me, April."

"I do, too. And I promise, I'll come visit."

"No, you won't, you're just saying that," I pouted.

"I will. I promise."

"When?"

As I was talking, April had stopped responding. I wasn't paying attention because I was too busy running my mouth.

"You hear what I said?" I asked again.

I had my back turned to April and could not see that she was having breathing issues. When I faced her to get her attention, I could see that she was trying to talk, but she just couldn't catch her breath. Her motor skills were shutting down, and things were happening fast. She collapsed on the bed and her eyes were blinking very slow, as if she were trying to remain conscious. The next thing I knew, she had passed completely out. I ran to her and I tried to revive her by slapping her face, but she was out.

"APRIL?!" I started to scream hysterically, "MISS BLAKE! MISTER BLAKE! DA-DDY!"

We rushed April to the hospital, and she was stabilized, but still unconscious. The doctors told us she could be sleep for hours, days, or weeks. There was no way that my dad and I were going to leave the next day, so we prepared to stay for a little while longer. Fortunately, it was only a matter of hours. When April woke up, she was surrounded by people who loved her. Mr. and

Mrs. Blake, and me and my dad, were sitting beside April's bed when she woke up.

"Look, she's awake dear," Mrs. Blake said to Mr. Blake.

"Thank, God," Mr. Blake said, as he sighed in relief.

"You gave us quite a scare, young lady," Mrs. Blake rubbed April's forehead.

"I'm sorry, I don't know what happened to me."

"Your insulin was very low. Have you been taking your medication as prescribed?" Mrs. Blake asked.

"No, I'm sorry. I've been feeling so good lately. I guess I thought I could miss a few doses."

"Well, you're better now and that's all that matters," Mr. Blake reassured April.

"You scared me so bad," I said nervously.

"I'm sorry, lil' sister."

When I looked in April's face, I knew I couldn't leave her. I loved my dad, but my dad didn't need me, April did. I felt that she would die without me.

"Daddy, can I talk to you for a minute?"

"Sure, baby," Daddy said.

Daddy and I walked into the hallway.

"Dad, what I'm about to ask you is very, very, important to me, OK?"

"Everything OK, sweetheart?"

"Dad, can April come live with us?"

"You're kidding, right?"

"No, Daddy, I'm very serious."

"She can't come live with us, Kiera. We don't even know her."

"I know her, Daddy, and if she doesn't come live with us, she's going to die."

"You're being a little dramatic, don't you think?"

"Daddy, no. The Blakes are going back to England and when they do, April is going to have to go back to the custody of the state."

"Look, I'm sorry about your friend, but I can't take in a complete stranger. I already have your sister, her child and you to take care of. Bringing in an extra person with health issues is completely out of the question."

"But, Daddy, what if everybody woulda' thought the same way about me?

"I'm sorry, sweetheart."

I looked at my dad with tears in my eyes and he hugged me. I hugged him back and then I walked back into April's room and sat beside her.

—

"I knew my dad wasn't going to leave April behind," I said with a big grin on my face.

"So, he did take in April?"

"Yes, and she became his daughter just like Khloe and me."

195

"I would like to meet April."

"I don't think that would be a problem at all, Dr. Turner."

"Good," Dr. Turner smiled, "I look forward to seeing you both next week, Kiera."

CHAPTER NINE

The year of 2020...

When I entered Dr. Turner's reception area, I thought it would be for the last time. I felt that she had done all that she could do for Khloe, Kiera and me, and collectively, we were all in a better mental space. This visit was all about April. It was her turn to find the peace that my other daughters and I had found.

I entered Dr. Turner's office first, while April remained behind in the reception area. I walked in and immediately noticed that Dr. Turner did not seem like her regularly poised and calm self. Her eyes were puffy. Her normally immaculate hair was out of place. She had a cup on her desk that was filled with something other than coffee. I was surprised to say the least.

"Dr. Turner?" I asked in surprise.

"Mr. Simms? How are you?"

"I'm great," I said, looking around and noticing books and other items were out of place. "Is everything, alright?"

"Yes…yes, everything is fine. Why do you ask?"

"I…uh…just wondering."

"No, no, say what's on your mind, Mr. Simms."

"Is today a good day for you? I could come back on another day if you like?"

"No! Today is fine."

"Are you sure?" I asked.

"Positive," Dr. Turner pointed to a chair. "Have a seat, Mr. Simms."

"Actually, I have my daughter outside."

"Which daughter?"

"April? You asked me to bring her in for this session, remember?"

"Yes...right, right. Send her in, please."

"Sure, I'll get her."

I went to the reception area and gestured for April to come into Dr. Turner's office. She stood up and followed me.

"Dr. Turner, this is my daughter April."

Dr. Turner's jaws nearly dropped to the floor at the sight of my daughter, "WOW! How are you, April?"

"I'm fine. How are you?"

"I'm...I'm...I'm here," Dr. Turner tried to smile unsuccessfully.

"Well, I'm going to let you ladies talk," I said. "I'll be sitting in the reception area until you're finished, April, alright?"

"Alright."

I walked out of Dr. Turner's office and patiently waited for April, while the two of them acquainted themselves.

"Forgive me for staring at you, April, but you are a total contrast from how I pictured you."

"Did you think I was obese?' April asked.

"To be honest, yes."

"I am no longer that person, inside or out."

"Can you tell me about your relationship with your father?'

"I adore my dad. He literally saved my life. Even though I was not his child biologically, he stepped in, loved me and treated me like I was his very own blood. As a matter of fact, he did for me what most men won't do for their own biological children. I love him for that."

"How is your relationship with your sisters?"

"We fight. We argue. We get on each other's nerves to no end, but we will also walk through fire for one another."

"Tell me about you. How was your upbringing? How was your childhood?"

"My childhood was pure hell…"

—

I was born in Compton, California to a crackhead mother and a criminal father. I was diagnosed at birth with the Human Immunodeficiency Virus, more commonly known as HIV. I've been in and out of hospitals my entire life. When I wasn't in hospitals, I was in foster care and adoption agencies. No one really wanted me because I was a fat kid with all sorts of health issues. I mean, I was grossly obese. I felt like a sideshow act whenever I was in public. People were always staring at me. The families that I lived with were sometimes good to me and sometimes very, very bad to me. I developed a mental defensive mechanism to block out all of the negativity and managed to escape to a place of positivity in my mind. I became immune to the ugliness shown towards me, and I decided that I would love everybody even if they didn't want to love me back. That was my childhood.

When I was fourteen, once again I became a ward of the court. By then, I had been there so many times that some of the tenured employees knew me very well, and they would take care of me beyond their job description. Some even took me home for the holidays, to spend time with them and their families. But it was only so much they could do. As strange as it may seem, I almost convinced myself that my childhood was no different from any other child's. Almost, but not quite.

After I turned fifteen, I was told that I had an interview with a family called the Blakes. I had been to many interviews, so I knew the routine-- sit down, talk, the foster parents get my hopes up, and then I never hear from them again. The Blakes were different. They walked in with smiles on their faces, just like all the previous potential foster care parents. But unlike most, they didn't stop smiling when they saw me. Their smiles grew broader.

"Hi, April, we're the Blakes, how are you?" Mr. Blake asked.

"I'm doing good. How are you?" I replied. I was thrown aback by their British accents.

We sat and talked for a while. I was impressed with the Blakes because they asked me a lot of questions about my future. They didn't ask one question about my past. Not that they didn't care, but they knew there was nothing they could do about my past, so they focused on what they knew they could do. Then out of nowhere, I heard what I thought I would never hear again.

"How would you like to come live with us for a while?" Mrs. Blake asked.

I was in shock. My immediate thought was that these weirdos were freaky pedophiles, or they wanted my organs. They would

have been awfully disappointed when they found out my body was infected with the HIV virus.

"Go home with you?" I chuckled, "Yeah, right."

"You don't think we're a good fit for you?" Mrs. Blake asked humbly.

"A good fit for you? Why would you want me to come live with you?'

"Why wouldn't we?" Mr. Blake replied sincerely.

"Look at me," I said, as I stood up.

"What does how you look have to do with you coming to live with us, April?" Mrs. Blake reached across the table and squeezed my hand gently. "From what we have heard about you, and from what we have seen of you, you are a brilliant young lady. All that we care about is providing you with a home and an opportunity for you to be the best you, you can be."

"Are you serious?" I was beginning to allow myself to believe that maybe they did want me to live with them.

"Dead serious," Mr. Blake smiled and nodded affirmation.

"I don't know what to say."

"Just say yes," Mrs. Blake said.

"Yes!" I could no longer hide my excitement. I suppose on the outside, I didn't reflect my feelings. On the outside, I didn't smile or show any emotion.

"Then I guess that's that." Mr. Blake said firmly.

I didn't find out that the Blakes had another foster child living with them until after I arrived at their home. Her name was

Kiera, and she was a couple of years younger than me. She was from Compton, and was black like me, so we had a lot in common. Our first interaction did not go so swimmingly, but from that moment on, we became sisters. The day after I arrived, Kiera and I were the only ones at home, and I was getting a snack from the refrigerator. When she walked in the kitchen, she didn't speak, she just stopped abruptly and stared at me. I had seen that look a million times, and I knew it was not a good thing. Since she was staring at me, I stared at her.

"What's wrong?" I asked.

"Huh?" Kiera replied.

"Why are you staring at me?" I asked.

"I wasn't staring. I was just looking."

"What's the difference?"

"I mean, you're in the kitchen so it's kind of hard for me to miss you."

"Really? Is that supposed to be a joke about my weight?" I asked.

"No. What does your weight have to do with anything?" Kiera chuckled, pissing me off.

"'I mean, you're in the kitchen so it's kind of hard for me to miss you,' isn't that what you just said?" I repeated, mocking Kiera.

"Yeah, that's what I said, but who said I was saying that because of your weight? I woulda' asked that about anybody."

"Really?" I said sarcastically.

"Yeah."

"OK, girl. Whatever."

"No, don't whatever me. I wasn't talking about your weight. I mean, it's just you and me in here. So, of course, I'm gon' see you," I could tell that Kiera was becoming a little pissed, too, so I tried to deescalate the situation.

"OK, if you say so. It's just, whatever," I said nonchalantly.

"Why you keep sayin' that?" Kiera was becoming more frustrated.

"It's no big deal. I'm overweight. I'mma big girl. I know it. It's cool. I know people stare at me and talk about me. I'm used to it."

"But don't that hurt your feelings?" Kiera asked.

"It used to. But now I'm just like, whatever, man."

"I wish I was like you."

"Really?" I asked. "Why?"

"Because I'm not like most girls, and when people find out my little secret, it's like they call me names and I can't stand that shit. I'm still the same person. It's just that I like…well, that's irrelevant. I'm still the same person."

"Go on and say it, you like girls. Ain't nothin' wrong with that."

"How did you know?" Kiera chuckled.

"It doesn't take a rocket scientist to figure out that you're not into boys. If that's your preference, then hey, do you."

"Do you think the Blakes know I like girls?"

"Uh, a-hell no. Those people don't have a clue about anything, other than Malibu and saving the world from all of its problems."

"They're good people, though," Kiera said. "I'm glad to have them as foster parents."

"They're the best. I don't think my mother knows who my father was. She was an addict and didn't want me, so I kept ending up back in the system, being rejected and neglected because nobody else wanted me either."

"Wow, I went through the same with my mother. She was hooked, too, and I had to take care of my little brother and sister until the children's services called the cops on my ass. They split us up and I don't know where they are."

"Dam, at least it was just me. So, how do you cope with not being able to see your kid brother and sister?"

"That shit is hard. As much as I used to hate having to take care of them all the time, I miss them so much. I've been trying to reach my daddy so he can come get me."

"You got a daddy?"

"Yeah, everybody got a daddy. They may not be there, but they exist."

"Right," I chuckled. "You don't have your father's number?"

"It was in my mama's phone. I had it wrote down, too. But when they took us to child services, I couldn't go home and get shit, so I don't know how to contact him. And he doesn't know where the hell I am," Kiera said sadly.

"Are you and your dad close?" I asked.

"Oh my God, yes," Kiera said. "I love my daddy so much. He come out here just to see me, and then I go see him in Atlanta."

"Where's your mom?"

"I don't know. When she on that shit she just leaves and then come back whenever she comes down. She probably been back to the house and found out that child services done took us. She probably ain't even trying to find us."

Just as we were bonding, the Blakes walked into the kitchen. I could tell by the looks on their faces that they were not in the best of moods.

"Girls," Mr. Blake said. "I think we have a problem. Nothing that can't be fixed, but it's a problem just the same."

"As Mr. Blake and I were getting packages out of the back seat of the car, we happened to notice this on the floor," Mrs. Blake held a joint in her hand and raised it in the air. "We are in tune with society, and we know that marijuana is now a recreational pastime, or a medicinal treatment. But it should still be used properly and accordingly with, or by adult supervision, when it comes to minors."

"So, who does this belong to?" Mr. Blake asked.

I looked at Kiera and then she looked at me. I knew the joint didn't belong to me, but I felt that I should take responsibility because I could deal with the Blakes better than Kiera. Not to mention, I did have a medicinal marijuana card.

"I'm sorry, Mr. and Mrs. Blake. It's mine. I didn't realize it had fell out. I should have told you that I use for medicinal purposes to help with my pain."

"Ohhhh," Mrs. Blake hugged me. "Oh, we didn't mean to come off harsh or insensitive. We didn't know, sweetheart."

"We owe you an apology, April. We should not have come off as accusatory. We should have simply inquired as to why you were using, instead of trying to find out who was using."

"It was a matter of miscommunication, that's all. Thank you for caring enough to ask," that went much better than I thought it would.

Later that night, Kiera came to my bedroom and knocked on my door.

"Come in," I answered.

Kiera walked in while I was connected to my ventilator.

"Whoa, what's that?" Kiera asked.

"A breathing machine to help me breathe at night when I sleep," I answered.

"Do you have to use this every night?"

"Yup, and sometimes during the day."

"I bet that sucks."

"It doesn't suck as much as being dead," I responded sarcastically.

"I feel you."

Kiera was standing silently as if she had more to say, "So, what's up?"

"Thank you for not snitching on me, and for taking the hit for that joint."

"Don't worry about it. That's what big sisters do."

"Big sisters? You wanna' be my big sister?" Kiera responded with surprise.

"Look, we don't have a choice, we're in this together. Blood don't always make you family. Situations, circumstances and love, do. We're sisters," I said confidently.

"Sisters, huh?" Kiera asked with a big smile on her face.

"Yup," I said as I went back to my comfortable position. "But for right now, can this sister get a little time to herself? I got a little somethin'-somethin' goin' on right now."

"OK, bet," Kiera laughed and then left my room. From that moment on, we were sisters.

We did everything together for the remainder of our school year, and we really had a family going on with the Blakes, but I knew that Kiera was really hurting to see her father. Fortunately for her and unfortunately for me, spending a lot of time in the system, I learned how to research missing families. I put my skills to use and found her dad. The school year was about up, and we were about to be returned to the state because the Blakes were returning to Europe. So, it was perfect timing. For her anyway.

The day Kiera's father arrived to pick her up, she was excited, as she should be. But when that reality hit that she was leaving-leaving, the sadness was so real, I literally passed out.

"This is a whole lot of shit for somebody who came here with nothing," Kiera joked.

"I'm saying," I joked back. "When did you have time to hoard all this stuff, girl?"

"I don't even know, but I got it! It's mine! And I'm keeping it!"

"Come here," I reached out my arms and Kiera started to cry and ran into my arms. "You big baby, what are you crying for?"

"I'm gonna' miss you."

"I'm gonna' miss you, too. But it's OK, you're going to Atlanta with your dad."

"I wish you could come with me, April."

"I do, too. And, I promise, I'll come visit."

"No, you won't, you're just saying that," Kiera pouted.

"I will. I promise."

"When?"

As Kiera was talking, I started to feel dizzy. I had been weak and tired all day. I thought it was just a spell that would pass, and that I would get over it, but it wasn't.

"You hear what I said?" Kiera asked again.

Kiera had her back turned and could not see that I was having issues. I could hear Kiera talking, and I was trying to respond, but I couldn't. My motor skills were shutting down, and it was all happening so fast. I flopped on the bed, and I was trying to remain conscious, but then everything went black. When Kiera noticed that I was not responding, she then turned and faced me. By that time, I had passed out.

"APRIL?!" Kiera screamed. She ran to me and tried to revive me by slapping my face. Then she started to scream hysterically, "MISS BLAKE! MISTER BLAKE! DA-DDY!"

—

When I regained consciousness, I was lying in a hospital bed with tubes running in and out of my body. The first person I saw was Kiera. She was sitting very uncomfortably in a chair next to me, holding my hand. Mr. and Mrs. Blake were snuggled together in another chair, and Mr. Simms was sitting in a folding chair. All of them were asleep. I squeezed Kiera's hand and she woke up.

"You know you didn't have to scare us like that. All you had to say was that you couldn't live without me and you wanted me to stay."

"Would you?" I whispered faintly.

"Nope," Kiera snapped back.

"See," I smiled.

Mrs. Blake heard us and woke up. She nudged Mr. Blake and woke him up, "Look, she's awake, dear."

"Thank God," Mr. Blake said.

The Blakes hugged and kissed me and then held my other hand. The Blakes had always made me feel like their family. However, I knew that it was only temporary. For the first time in my life, I realized what it felt to be able to trust that no matter what happened, I always had a family who was going to love me.

"You nearly scared us to death, sweetheart," Mrs. Blake said as she rubbed my head.

"Yes, you gave us quite a scare, young lady."

"I'm sorry, I don't know what happened to me," I said.

"Your insulin was very low. Have you been taking your medicine?" Mrs. Blake asked.

"No, I'm sorry. I've been feeling so good lately."

"You've been feeling good because you've taken as prescribed," Mr. Blake added.

"Daddy, can I talk to you for a minute?" Kiera asked her father.

"Sure, baby," Mr. Simms said.

"We'll be right back," Kiera said. Mr. Simms followed her out of my hospital room and into the hall.

"You know the worst thing about being sick, Mr. and Mrs. Blake?" I asked.

"What's that, dear?" Mrs. Blake asked back.

"Being too poor and too young to pay the bills."

"You don't ever have to worry about any bills, April," Mr. Blake smiled. "Ever!"

"What do you mean, Mr. Blake?"

"Your hospital bills are taken care of, and they will be for as long as you need it."

"I know I'm still a teenager, Mr. Blake, but I know bills have to be paid."

"You are our family, April. Just because we have to go back home, it doesn't mean that you are no longer our responsibility. OK?" Mrs. Blake asked.

I became overwhelmed at that time and I began to cry, "Why are you doing this for me? What have I done for you to be this kind to me?"

"You loved us as your parents. You didn't care about our race. You didn't care about our culture. You didn't have to do that, but you did. You are full of love and you were the perfect child to us." Mrs. Blake said. "You see, we wanted to have children for a long time. When we were finally blessed to have children, we had a perfect little girl. Unfortunately, God didn't give us a lot of time with her. She died when she was just three years old. You and Kiera have filled a void in our lives that we thought we could never find again. You will always be our daughter for as long as you want us to be your parents."

"I want you to be my parents forever."

"And we will," Mr. Blake said.

The Blakes bent over and hugged me. While we were still embraced in our hug, Kiera burst through the door of my hospital room, "Guess what, April? My dad said you can come live with us when the Blakes return to Europe!"

"Huh?" I responded with confusion.

"You're coming to live with us in Atlanta!"

"Did she bump her head, Mr. Simms?" I asked.

"My daughter can be very convincing when she wants to be," Mr. Simms said with a smile.

"What's this, she say?" Mrs. Blake asked.

"If April wants, she can come live with us in Atlanta. My daughter is not willing to leave without her, so here we are. I imagine there are a lot of legal steps in the process, but I'm willing to do what's necessary to make it happen."

"I have to ask my parents," I looked at Mr. and Mrs. Blake, "So what do you think?"

"I think it's a marvelous situation," Mrs. Blake said joyfully.

"Our prayers have been answered," Mr. Blake responded. "We wanted you to end up in a safe and comfortable environment, and what better place than to be with your sister."

"Why would you let a perfect stranger move into your home, Mr. Simms?" I asked.

"If my daughter loves you the way that she does, then I will have no problem loving you, too, because that's how much I love my child. Don't get me wrong, it'll take some adjustments, but like Mr. Blake said, I'd feel better knowing that you are safe and sound. What better way of knowing that than to have you under my roof."

"Thank you so much, Mr. Simms, but I feel like I'm imposing on you. You and Kiera are just reuniting. You don't mind me being in the way?"

"Girl, please. Can't nobody get in the way of me and my daddy," Kiera chuckled and hugged Mr. Simms.

"Isn't this the same situation we created last year with our family, dear?" Mrs. Blake asked.

"Yes," I smiled, "I just don't want to be a problem for them, that's all."

"We'll be fine," Mr. Simms said.

In a year's time, my life had gone from an unforgettable nightmare to unbelievable fairytale. Not only did I have one parent. I had three. I said my goodbye to Kiera and Mr. Simms that night, and they flew to Atlanta the following morning. A few weeks later, I flew to Atlanta with the Blakes and we spent time together with Kiera. We all said our very tearful goodbyes as the Blakes flew back home across the big pond, and I began my new life in the city of Atlanta, Georgia.

—

Kiera and I picked up where we left off in Malibu as loving sisters. We met our third sister, and we blended very quickly, as if we had known each other our entire lives. Khloe was a year older than me, so we had a little more in common than Kiera and me. Kiera would sometimes get jealous of us when we talked about things above her head. But the jealousy didn't last long. She loved being the baby sister, even if she was only two or three years younger than us.

Although my sisters and I did a lot of things together, my weight and health issues hindered my mobility. They never complained or judged me, but I could tell that there were things that they wanted to do that they knew my body would not allow. Mr. Simms and Kiera would never have discussed this subject with me because they loved me too much. However, my sister Khloe did not avoid discussing it with me, because she loved me too much.

"How do you feel, sister?" Khloe asked.

"You know, I have good days and bad days."

"You know if you lost that weight you would be in much better shape, don't you?"

"Dam! Like that, Khloe?"

"I'm sorry, but I love you and I don't want to see you sit up here and die, when there's something we can do to prevent it."

"We?" I asked.

"Yeah!" Khloe said sternly. "We!"

"Well, what can we do, Ms. Khloe?"

"One, we can change your eating habits. Two, we can start exercising together. Three, you can have gastric bypass surgery."

"What is that?"

"It's a surgery to help overweight people get rid of weight quick."

"They're not going to let me have that surgery, Khloe."

"Why not? You got the money. Between your white parents and daddy, they will take care of your surgery like it's nothing."

"I know that, but did you forget that I have HIV?"

"No, but with today's technology, you can't tell me that people with HIV can't have gastric bypass surgery. I don't believe that for a minute."

"Well, I'm telling you."

"So, you're saying that we can't find you somebody who will do that surgery on you?"

"Yup."

"Girl, you crazy as hell, watch me."

"OK, I'm watching."

I didn't have to watch for too long. A few days later Khloe and Kiera came into my room with Mr. Simms.

"What?" I asked with curiosity, looking at all three of them.

"Don't ask me," Mr. Simms said. "I don't have a clue. They pushed me in here."

"We have a surgery for you called sleeve gastrectomy," Khloe said. "It's for overweight people with HIV."

"What?" Mr. Simms asked. "What the hell are you talking about, Khloe?"

"April needs surgery to save her life, Daddy, and we found a safe surgery for her that can do it."

"Whoa! Whoa! Whoa! Slow down. What is this all about?"

"We want April to get better, but in order for her to get better, she has to get this surgery, Daddy," Kiera added on.

"How much is this surgery, April?" Mr. Simms asked.

"I have no idea, Mr. Simms, they did this on their own."

"It cost from eight thousand dollars to twenty thousand dollars," Khloe said.

"That ain't nothing for you and the Blakes, Daddy."

"The hell it ain't!" Mr. Simms shouted. "Twenty thousand dollars? I don't have twenty thousand dollars laying around the house like that."

"The Blakes said they would help," Kiera said.

"How do you know they would help, Kiera?"

"I asked them, Daddy."

"So y'all have this all planned out?"

"Yup!" Kiera said quickly.

217

"Let's do this," Mr. Simms said, pointing at Kiera and Khloe, "you two get out. I need to talk to April alone."

"Really, Daddy?" Khloe said, putting her hands on her hips.

"Really, now get your ass out."

"You are such a mean man, Daddy," Kiera said on her way out of the door.

"That's, OK, out!"

Kiera and Khloe left, leaving Mr. Simms and me alone. Over my first year with him, we had a lot of alone time and we talked a lot, so we were accustomed to sharing special moments. This moment, as important and life changing as it was, was no different from any of the others.

"So, what do you think about this surgery, April?"

"It doesn't matter to me."

"No, sweetheart, it has to matter to you. This is your life. This is your health. You can't be nonchalant on this one. Do you want this surgery?"

"I...I...I...kinda' do, but I'm scared."

"What are you afraid of?"

"What if it doesn't work? What if something happens?"

"It's OK. It's alright to be scared," Mr. Simms said. "But if you think this surgery can help your health, and this is what you want to do, I will support you one hundred percent."

"Really?" I was excited but then I quickly calmed down when I considered the price. "That's a lot of money, Mr. Simms. But they said the Blakes would help."

"If we need the Blakes we can ask them, but I think we can handle it without them," Mr. Simms smiled. "So, are we doing it?"

"Yes! We are doing it!" I hugged Mr. Simms. "Thank you so much, Mr. Simms."

"Don't you think it's time you put the Mr. Simms to bed? You're my legally adopted daughter. You are my child."

"What do you want me to call you?"

"How about you call me what the rest of these knuckleheads call me? Daddy. After all, you're my favorite anyway," Mr. Simms winked at me as he walked out of the room.

From that moment on, Mr. Simms officially became my dad.

CHAPTER TEN

The summer of 2011...

T he surgery was a major success, and I entered my senior year of high school as a new person. I received more attention than I wanted. Initially, I enjoyed it, but then I noticed the hypocrisy of my classmates. When I was obese, nobody wanted to be my friend. But after my surgery, I couldn't push people away. After I graduated from high school, I followed my sister to Spelman. When Khloe attended grad school at Howard University, I followed her there as well, for my graduate degree. It took me five years to get out of there because I took some time off to travel and model. That put Kiera only a year behind me. Kiera skipped Spelman altogether and went directly to Howard as an undergrad. So, the three sisters had relocated to Washington D.C. I will never forget the first day I arrived.

"Oh my God! I'm so happy to see you!" I shouted.

"How was your flight?" Khloe asked.

"It was looooong," I said. "I didn't think that I was ever going to get here."

"Well you're here now, so let's get lit."

Khloe helped me with my luggage, and I asked about Kiera, "Where's Kiera?"

"She had an exam. She'll get up with us later."

"How are her grades?"

"Better," Khloe laughed. "I had to get in that ass, but she's hittin' those books now."

"Good, because I already had my big sister speech ready."

"Like I said," Khloe said, "that ass done already been handled. Daddy is spending all of that money on her education and she's up here bullshitting."

I always admired Khloe for being tough, straightforward and direct with everybody, including her sisters. Although she loved us beyond words, she didn't let us get away with anything. When I heard that Kiera was screwing up, I knew that it was only a matter of time before the mother hen started quacking. Khloe and I went to lunch, while we waited for Kiera to meet us at the restaurant.

"This girl dam near flunked out of school stayin' up all night strippin' and shit, talkin' about she strippin' her way through college, like Daddy's not payin' for her tuition. I believe that strippin' is what turned her on to girls," Khloe said.

"Naw, sis. She liked girls back when she was thirteen. But that's her thing, so if she likes it, I love it."

"I don't like it. I'm not homophobic, but that's just not my lifestyle."

"And that's cool, Khloe. But we have to let Kiera love and live her own life the way she wants, in order for her to be happy."

"I don't give a shit about her happiness!" Khloe and I laughed out loud. "I want her to stay my little baby sister forever."

"You two needy ass girls drive me crazy going back and forth. I'm always the middleman. Some time, you all make me want to scream."

"You're the middle sister. We're supposed to drive your ass crazy, April."

"Seriously though, I can't thank you enough for getting me this job at the Capitol Building, big sister. It's my dream job."

"If there's anyone I can vouch for with confidence, it's you, little sister. How 'bout a toast to the Simms sisters' reunion and you getting your dream job, April."

"I'll drink to that!" I said.

We laughed and drank a couple of glasses of wine so that we could be in the right frame of mind for Little Miss Thang. When she arrived, she sashayed her way over to our table, waving and switching her hips way too much to be entering a restaurant.

"Look at that thang, April," Khloe said, shaking her head.

Kiera could not see us watching her strut through the restaurant like a movie star, but we could see her, much to our chagrin. When she saw me sitting at the table with Khloe, she hurried her way over to me.

"Hey, ba-beeee!" Kiera said, hugging me. "Welcome to Chocolate City!"

"You know we need to talk, right?" I said rhetorically.

"Oh shit, what did Khloe tell you?"

"Never mind that. What are you doing in school? Are you graduating?"

"Yo! Hold up! One question at a time."

"How did you do on your exam today?" I asked.

"Killed it."

"What are you going to do now that you're out of school?" Khloe asked.

"I don't know, probably get a job."

"Get a job doing what?"

"I don't know, just work, Khloe."

"You're not considering going back home?" I asked.

"For what? I'm going to take some time off and spend time with my baby."

"You can spend time with your baby anytime. I think somebody needs to go be with Daddy for a while. Something's wrong with him," I said.

"What's wrong with, Daddy?" Kiera asked, with sincere concern.

"Did you all know that Daddy has been seeing a therapist for years?"

"Who's daddy?" Khloe asked curiously.

"Your daddy!" I responded.

"Why?" Kiera asked.

"I don't know, but before I left, he asked me to go with him."

"Did you say yes or no?" Khloe asked.

"I told him I would think about it. I really haven't made up my mind yet," I said. "He told me he was going to ask you all, too."

"Oh, hell naw!" Kiera blurted out. "I'm not going to talk to no therapist."

"If Daddy wants us to talk to a therapist, we're talking to a therapist." Khloe said.

"You really do think you're somebody mama, don't you?" Kiera said jokingly. "Well let me tell you something, mama, I ain't going to see no dam psychiatrist. My head messed up enough as it is."

"All of your lesbian activity and what not is what messed up yourhead," Khloe joked.

"You need to find you a woman and get off my ass, mama."

"I'm strictly-dickly, baby."

"You two are nuts!" I laughed. "You two never seem to hurt each other's feelings when you actin' a fool."

"She knows better, April," Khloe said.

"I know I ain't thinkin' about your Mommy Dearest ass," Kiera said. "By the way, I need a place to stay for a while."

"You wait until April gets here to tell me that you need a place to stay, Kiera?"

"Obviously, I didn't know I would need a place to stay until now," Kiera replied. "Me and my baby are having problems. That's why we need some time alone to work this out."

"You can come stay with me on one condition, Kiera."

"Dam, what's the condition?"

"You have to support Daddy in his therapy."

"What? I don't wanna' see no therapist, Khloe."

"Why not? What are you afraid of finding out, Kiera?' I asked.

"Look y'all, my childhood was hell, all of our childhoods were. Why would we wanna' bring all of that shit back up?"

"Because the man who saved us from that hell may be going through hell himself. Are you saying that for our own selfish reasons, we shouldn't be there for him?' Khloe asked.

"That's not what I'm saying, and you know it, Khloe. I'm scared. That's all. I'm just scared of opening Pandora's box."

"We're all going to do it, so if we open Pandora's box, then we'll deal with it as a family," Khloe assured Kiera.

"OK, Khloe, but you go first and tell us how it went," Kiera suggested.

"Cool. I'll call Daddy and let him know," Khloe turned to me and said, "you're in right, little sister?"

"Whatever we need to do to help Daddy, I'll do it," I said it and I meant it.

"Now listen to me, Kiera, when you get a job, once you get your first check, we are immediately finding an apartment. I can't have both of you sleeping on my furniture."

"Don't worry, I gets down and I don't need my sisters all up in my business."

"And what business is that, baby sister?" I asked.

"Listen to your sanctified ass trying to get all up in my business," Kiera laughed. "I mean sex! Loud! Yelling! Screaming! Hot sex!"

"Oh my God!" I said, embarrassed.

"Shiiiiiit, I got to get it in!" Kiera laughed.

"Do you have sex a lot, Kiera?" I asked.

"As much as I can!"

"She's a little freak," Khloe joked.

"I ain't denying shit!"

"I guess I'm missing out then," I added.

"You have no idea."

Although I may have sounded naive to Khloe and Kiera, it was only because I was. Despite my outward metamorphosis from ugly duckling to beautiful swan, I still felt like the same unattractive, obese girl that was constantly criticized and traumatized. That is why I held on to my secret and kept it to myself. I was a twenty-four-year-old beautiful virgin with a frightening and an incurable deadly virus.

—

On our drive to Khloe's place, we did a lot of talking. Khloe knew so much about life for her twenty-five years of age. She was only a year older than me, but she was leaps and bounds ahead of me in experience. She was in full control of herself and her life. All three of us sisters had been through a lot as children, but Khloe used her past as a chip on her shoulder to succeed. And there was nothing, and I mean nothing, that intimidated her or deterred her from doing what she wanted to do. I wanted to be like my sister.

It took me a day or two to settle in, and then Khloe started to prepare me for my job, which was still two weeks away. I was excited about my new life, and I could not wait to get started. After the first week of job training, I was released to the wild to

226

fend for myself. The Capitol Building is not a place for the weak or meek. In a way, I was both. However, Khloe had readied me for the challenge, no matter what came my way. Still, that first day kicked my ass!

"How was your first day?"

"Intimidating! Maybe this wasn't a good idea. I feel like I'm going to let you down, Khloe, and I don't want to do that."

"You're not going to let me down because I'm not going to let you let me down."

"But I don't know if I…"

"A'ight! Stop it! Enough of that self-pitying shit!" Khloe snapped. "It takes time to adjust, so start adjusting. Stop thinking so negatively, April. Look at you. You're gorgeous. You're smart as hell. You have to work on your confidence. I mean, you are feeling what I'm saying?"

"I feel you, but I can't change how I feel inside."

"How do you feel inside, April?"

"Inside, I feel like I'm still the fat chick that everybody finds repulsively disgusting."

"Let me tell you something, little sister. Even when you were overweight, you were beautiful. That's why we all love you. OK?"

"OK," I nodded.

On my second day as an employee on Capitol Hill, I was both thrilled and frightened simultaneously. Everyone has a definable moment in their life when something happens, and they know that they will never forget it. That definable moment for me was when I saw my new boss, the Leader of the Senate, Mr. Parker

Turner III. He was from Georgia, and I had seen him once when I was in high school. Since then, I have seen him on television, but I never thought I would ever actually see him again in real life. Nothing like that ever happens to me. I was not into politics, but I was into him because that was one fine white man.

I couldn't help staring at him as I passed him on the floor of the Lower House. The Lower House is the room where the House of Representatives meet to debate and vote. When I first glanced upon him, my eyes were embarrassingly transfixed. He was tall, handsome and fairly young, unlike the typical older members of Congress. The Senator stood about six feet and four inches tall. He had a square chin, and clean-shaven face, with jet black hair that was gray at his temples and sideburns. His shoulders were broad, and hips were narrow. His teeth were white and even across. He possessed such handsomely masculine features, that I was immediately captivated by the man, the happily married man.

An hour or so later, Khloe sent me on an errand to pick up a document from the Senator. She described my role as the Senator's page girl, and said my job was to do whatever he wanted, whenever he needed. I could not believe I had landed such a prestigious job. I returned to drop off the Senator's document, but he wasn't there. I was told to deliver it directly into his hand, so I waited impatiently in his office. As I stood there, I gazed around the room admiring his accomplishments and imagining the journey that led him to the office of the Senate; awards, certificates and degrees covered the four walls of his office. My eyes paused when they came upon a picture sitting on his desk that showed the Senator and his children. His son looked to be close to my age. His oldest daughter looked to be in her mid-teens and the youngest daughter looked around ten years old.

I only meant to stare at the photo for a moment and then sit and wait for the Senator. However, my imagination held me captive and my feet decided to move on their own. I walked over to his desk and I picked up the picture of his children and imagined myself as the wife of a powerful man such as the Senator.

"May I help you?" the Senator spoke softly.

"Oh! I'm sorry," I quickly placed the picture back on his desk. "Good afternoon, sir! I am the new page and I was directed to assist you with…"

"What is your name?" The Senator interrupted.

"My name is April Simms."

"Good to meet you, uh, Ms. Simms. Now how may I help you?

"I am your new page and my sis…," I caught myself mid-sentence and changed my thought process. "I was directed to assist you in any way that you may need assistance, sir."

"Do you always speak as if you're giving a monologue for a theatrical audition?"

"Excuse me, sir?"

"Never mind," the Senator shuffled papers on his desk. "Can you please get me a cup of coffee?"

"Yes, sir."

I tended to the Senator's coffee and brought it back to him.

"Here you are, sir," I smiled as I handed him the scalding hot coffee.

The Senator sniffed the coffee and then handed it back to me. "What is this?"

"It's your coffee, sir," I smiled again. "I was told that you liked it strong, black, no sugar, no cream.

"Flora!" the Senator spoke in a voice that seemed too low for anyone outside of his office to hear. "Flora, get in here now!"

Flora Jourdain, the Senator's personal assistant, rushed into his office. Flora was tall, slender, blonde and all the way Caucasian. Her hair was cut short around the side and the back, with long bangs that covered her entire forehead. She wore thick black rimmed glasses.

"How may I help you, Mr. Senator?"

"Please instruct Ms. Simms on how I would like my coffee in the morning."

"Yes, sir," Flora said. "Come with me."

I followed Flora to a file cabinet. She opened the bottom drawer that read, "The Daniel's File." She looked at me and then smiled as she pulled out a bottle of Jack Daniel's whiskey. She poured a cap full into the Senator's cup of coffee.

"That should do it."

"You mean the Senator drinks Jack Daniel's in his coffee?"

"He likes his coffee very particular," Flora chuckled as she put the bottle back in the drawer. "Particular, meaning it must have this particular secret ingredient to make it taste just right."

"So, am I supposed to put Jack Daniel's in his coffee every morning?"

"Yes, if you want to continue to be a page for the Senator."

"Oh my God, who knew?" I joked.

"Actually, he's quite normal in comparison to the rest of the whackos here on the Hill. Considering his counterparts, he's a pretty good Senator to work for."

"I guess I better get this to him before his coffee gets cold."

"Trust me, that Jack Daniel's will keep that coffee lit up for a while."

I took the coffee back to the Senator, and he moved the cup from side to side as he sniffed its aroma.

"Ah! Perfect."

"Is there anything else I can do for you, sir?"

"Yes," the Senator said. "Disappear."

"Oh, OK, please let me know if you need me for anything," I opened the door to leave when the Senator called me to his desk.

"Ms. Simms?"

"Yes, sir," I stopped in my tracks.

"Have you ever voted?"

"No, sir."

"Why not?" the Senator asked.

"Because I never really had a candidate that I wanted to vote for."

"I see," the Senator contemplated momentarily and then said, "if you were to vote, who would you vote for? Republican or Democrat?"

"Well, I was raised as a Democrat."

"I'm not understanding your position, Ms. Simms," the Senator said. "Does that mean you would vote Democrat because your family votes Democrat?"

"If I say that I voted Democrat will I get to keep my job?" I said sarcastically.

"Your job is not in danger, Ms. Simms. But your character very well may be," the Senator smiled. "How do you feel about being a Liberal but working for a Conservative?"

"I think that so long as I am not forced to vote one way or the other, it will be a great opportunity for me to learn how our government operates. I need to know about our government because there are laws that need to be changed."

"Which laws are you referencing, Ms. Simms?"

"Medical laws!" I said sternly. "People are dying! They are in need of medical attention, but they can't afford to pay for it. I was one of them."

"I'm sorry to hear that," the Senator said sincerely. "But what do you think the government should do about that?"

"Help us, sir."

"I used to think the same way as you when I was your age, Ms. Simms. I used to think that I could change the entire world. But then I realized that I could not. I was then satisfied with perhaps changing the entire world of those that I could."

"I understand, sir."

"So, Ms. Simms, do you have any prior experience in politics?"

"No, not really, sir," I said.

"What college did you attend?"

I attended Spelman University."

"Spelman, huh?"

"Yes, sir."

"Hmm!" the Senator said. "That's my district and I'm quite proud of that school."

"Thank you, sir."

The Senator smiled at me and then proceeded to ask more questions. I was not exactly sure why he was inquiring so much about my life, but I was flattered that he would even take the time to talk to me.

"I have a question that I want you to answer and I want you to be totally honest with me."

"Yes, sir?"

"Why do you think my party has lost the past two presidential elections?"

"You want the truth, sir?"

"Yes, I want the truth."

"I think that the Republicans are disconnected from women's issues, and poor people and minorities in general. I think they feel that their money is more important than the issues. Sometimes the Republicans tend to have more money than sense."

"That stings. You do realize that I am a Republican, don't you?" the Senator joked.

"I'm sorry, sir."

"No need for an apology, Ms. Simms, I asked for the truth and you gave it to me," the Senator drank from his cup and then continued talking. "Is that why you're a Democrat? Because you think my party cares more about money than the issues?"

"Well, not exactly. I see the Democrats as a lesser of two evils. My issue with them is that they are too concerned about appearances. They want to appear that they care so much about the welfare of the people that they make unattainable promises that they can never keep."

"In the defense of Democrats and Republicans alike, despite the earnestness of our promises to the American people, it's difficult for any party to achieve an objective when their adversary is trying to achieve an opposing objective. It's not so much about not keeping a promise, as it is about getting your adversaries to vote your way. In most circumstances, getting an adversary to vote on your promise often means that they are voting against their own promise."

"I understand, sir. But like yourself, sir, the politicians that make these promises are aware of the opposition's objective before they make them. The American people are entitled to make an informed decision based on the potential of their candidate to fulfill their promise, not the promise itself. But the truth is so diluted we don't know what's the promise or the potential."

"Is there a difference?"

"There's definitely a difference. Potential has a ceiling of expectation. Promise is a guarantee of deliverance."

"You seem to be very knowledgeable of politics, Ms. Simms."

"I've always been fascinated with the political process, but I've never really been an active participant in the political process."

"I have a feeling you will. You have all of the makings. But if you do, don't let anyone convince you to lose that naivete of believing that we are here to be good or do good"

"Thank you, sir," I smiled, and he smiled back. "I want you to know that for now, I will do my best to be the best page you've ever had."

"Good."

I walked out of the Senator's office on cloud nine. I could not believe that he had actually taken the time to talk to me. The Senator was not a passing fascination for me; he was a permanent fixture of the prototypical husband that I had been looking forward to meeting since I was a little girl. When I walked out of the Senator's office, Khloe was standing there with a frown and her arms folded, tapping her feet.

"What the hell was that?" Khloe asked.

"What was what?"

"That friendly little conversation in there?"

"We were just talking."

"That wasn't just talking, April. Stay away from that man. He's married."

"I thought you told me to do whatever he wanted me to do whenever he wanted me to do it?'

"You know what I meant, April."

"Look, we were just talking politics. That's it!"

"Well, stop it! People watch everything you do around here. Trust me, you don't want to be that girl around here. Reputations like that can cost you your career."

"We only talked, Khloe. I promise."

"OK, April. Just watch yourself around here."

"I will...I promise. Now what would you like for me to do next?" I asked Khloe with great eagerness.

"Mr. Senator is hosting a very important meeting Thursday morning at eleven a.m., and I need you to order lunch for him and ten additional people. Oh, that should include beverages for all."

"From where do I order lunch?"

"Call this caterer," Khloe handed me a business card. "They should know the menu. Got it?'

"Yup. I think I have it."

"Are you sure?" Khloe asked.

"Positive."

"OK, little sister, go get 'em."

"I'm on it!"

The lunch went off without a hitch, and I was congratulated by Khloe and Flora for doing such a wonderful job. A few days passed before I would see the Senator again. He spent a lot of time in Georgia with his family, so he wasn't accessible every day. Whenever he came into the office, I was ecstatic. This particular morning, he came into the office to sign documents, which meant that I would get to talk to him while transferring his correspondence. I made sure that I positioned myself to talk to him, if only for a moment, before he left. I informed Flora that I would be preparing the Senator's coffee and taking it to him. She chuckled. I gathered she knew I was quite fond of him.

"Here's your coffee, sir," I handed the Senator his coffee.

He moved the cup from side to side beneath his nose and sniffed its aroma, and then he took a sip. "Perfect!"

"Glad you're pleased, sir. I like pleasing you."

"Oh really?" the Senator smiled seductively. "How would you like to be my guest for lunch, Ms. Simms?"

I was shocked. "I would absolutely love that, sir. Are you sure?"

"Clear my schedule and have Flora call 'Le Relais du Parc.' Oh, and have a car pick us up around noon."

"Sir, do I need to clear that we're going to lunch with Flora?"

"Clear it with Flora? Why would you have to clear anything with Flora? You work for me, Ms. Simms."

"Yes, sir," I nodded in agreement.

"I have to get back to signing these documents. Thanks for the coffee and I will see you at lunch."

"Yes, sir."

I made a straight line to Flora's desk to inform her of my lunch with the Senator. She seemed surprised, or should I say, disappointed, that she was not invited to the luncheon as well. That is when she demanded that I should report to her on any of my instructions that are handed down by the Senator. I respectfully explained to her that I did ask the Senator if I should inform her of our impromptu luncheon, and I repeated his response, verbatim.

She was not happy at all. I found Flora to be overprotective of the Senator. I tried to clarify to her that he and I were meeting only to discuss his upcoming election. I suppose she saw me as competition for his attention. She had no idea just how big of a competition I would become.

CHAPTER ELEVEN

The summer of 2020...

The Despite Flora's objection to my luncheon with the Senator, she kindly and thoroughly prepped me on some of the political terminology that I might have found useful. The most important term I needed to know at that time was "Car," which meant a limousine that Congress and dignitaries used for transportation. She also told me that whenever the car arrived for my luncheon with the Senator, I needed to be in it.

Flora arranged for the car to pick up the Senator and me around noon. The Senator was not at all concerned with spectators who watched as we walked side-by-side to the car, but I was. None of these people had ever seen or heard of me. Their understanding of my relationship with the Senator was completely unknown and could have been completely misinterpreted.

I tried to keep my eyes straight ahead and pay no attention to the gawkers, but the blatant stares made me uncomfortable. After all, the Senator was a married man. I was not accustomed to that type of interest from my peers, so receiving it from the important leaders that ran the greatest nation on earth only polarized my paranoia.

The driver met us at the limo and opened the door for us. He was a large, very muscular white man. He appeared to be middle-aged. He had both young and mature features. I would say he stood almost six feet and nine inches tall. He was a giant! He had an evenly tanned complexion. His head and face were clean-shaven, but his eyebrows were dark black and kind of bushy. His muscles bulged from his fitted black suit. He wore a white shirt with a black tie and black shoes. He wore black shades with black lenses. His name was Maize.

It was the first time I had ever ridden in a limousine and I was impressed. The Senator and I sat across from one another. He was on one side of the limo and I was on the other. He had the chauffeur raise the partition so that we could talk.

"So, are you curious to know why I asked you to lunch, Ms. Simms?" the Senator asked.

"I am very curious, sir."

"I find you to be an ambiguous enigma that I must comprehend."

"Me? An ambiguous enigma?" I asked sarcastically. "Why, I'm just a little ol' small town girl from Compton, California."

"You are hardly a mere anything from anywhere."

"I am what I am, sir, a product of my environment."

"Forgive my manners, Ms. Simms," the Senator held a glass in the air. "Do you indulge?"

"Yes, sir, I drink socially. But I think I'll pass on the drink for now."

"I never really understood the terms of 'social' or 'casual' drinkers to describe a person who drinks on occasion. Most of the people I've ever seen inebriated were at social or casual events. In my humble opinion, inebriated drunkards that attend social and casual events are social drinkers. Perhaps we should change the term to 'occasional' drinkers, or maybe even 'infrequent' drinkers," the Senator joked. "I just don't see the logic behind the aforementioned terminologies."

"If it's any consolation to you, sir, from now on, I will refer to myself as an infrequent drinker."

"Here's to infrequent drinkers everywhere, Ms. Simms!" the Senator lifted his glass for a toast.

As the Senator finished his sentence, the car pulled in front of the restaurant. I started to exit once the car came to a complete stop, but the Senator raised his hand, gesturing for me to sit still until the chauffeur opened the door. When we stepped out of the car, and I could get a detailed view of the restaurant, I was in awe. I stared at the outside of the building in amazement, as we patiently waited for the Secret Service to secure our dining area.

Hailing from Compton, I had never seen such an inimitably crafted restaurant. The outside was magnificently designed. I thought to myself, "if the interior complemented the exterior, then I was set for an afternoon of elegant delight." As soon as we stepped inside, I knew instantly that I would not be disappointed. The ambience and the food were of extravagant flavor.

I think the Senator selected that particular restaurant, because he knew I would be impressed. Despite my inner enthusiasm, I presented myself as a frequent connoisseur of such establishments. There I was, April Simms, eating lunch with one of the most powerful men in America. I felt like a princess in a fairytale dream. That was until we were escorted by the Senator's many Secret Servicemen to a private table, secluded from the other patrons.

"Sir, if you don't mind my mentioning, you sure have an abundance of security."

"My security is not wasted upon the unnecessary."

"Does that mean that your life is in danger?"

"That depends on what you perceive as danger," the Senator said. "I am a Senator of a political party and that translates to having many rivals, known and unknown. With any type of rivalry, comes forth the threat of danger."

"I never thought that politicians had such a dangerous job. Do you really believe that someone is trying to assassinate you, sir?"

"Let's just say that I believe that there are many of our fellow Americans in this vast country of ours that believe I would serve my country better as a corpse, rather than as a Senator."

"Do you fear your mortality, sir?"

"My demise, Ms. Simms, is inevitable. There is no reason for me to fear what I know is only the natural evolution of my cycle of existence. I am resolved to the fact that I cannot be the victor over death. But I can, and will, conquer my life by achieving the expectations placed upon me at my birth."

"Please forgive me for all of the questions, sir, but I am captivated by your life."

"I do not mind your questions. I believe that one never knows if one never asks."

"May I ask a few more questions?"

"Certainly."

"Do you have an idea of who your likely assassin could be?"

"It could be one or many. It could be my neighbor, my friend or my foe. It could be anyone," the Senator smiled. "It could even be you."

"I promise you, sir, I am not capable of harming a fly."

"When threatened, Ms. Simms, anyone is capable of harming anyone," the Senator peeked at his menu. "I think this topic is spoiling my appetite. I suggest that we shift our dialogue to a more pleasant discourse."

"I am in agreement, sir."

"If you need help with the menu, I am at your assistance."

"I think I will fare OK with the menu, sir," I offered a warm smile to the Senator and then opened my menu. "May I ask you one more question, sir?"

"Of course," the Senator said. "Consider this an open conversation, Ms. Simms. You don't need a prerequisite to ask a question."

"Why am I here, sir?"

"Why are you here?" The Senator sighed. "Hmm, good question. Well, you're here because I invited you. I invited you because I want to know more about you. I want to know more about you, so I can decide whether or not I want to make love to you.'

"Ex…excuse me, sir?"

"You heard me properly. You and I have an undeniable connection, and I want to make love to you."

"Forgive my confusion, sir, but I do not quite understand what you mean when you say that you want to make love to me. I understand the words, 'making love,' but I don't understand the correlation between those words and us."

"Perhaps," the Senator smiled. "I don't believe in coincidences or chance meetings, Ms. Simms. I believe in fate. I believe that there's a reason for everything. I believe that there's a reason why you came to work for me. Who really knows? Maybe you can learn from my experience? Maybe my office is just a crossroad to your next destination? Or maybe we were meant to make love. I don't know, but there is something magnetic between us. It's powerful! It's passionate! Whatever it is, it has to be resolved."

"Good luck with that, sir."

I was overwhelmed and intimidated at the same time. Contrarily, I wanted to throw myself on the table so that he could have his way with me as well. Whether I wanted to be there or not was beyond my control. We continued to talk during lunch, mostly about his family. He showed me another picture of his children and, one by one, told me a little about each of them. His oldest son, Parker, was twenty-one years old and a senior at Georgetown University. His oldest daughter, Madison, was sixteen, and an honor student at a prestigious private school. Madison was a brunette, slender and athletic. His daughter, Autumn, was eight. She was an adorable blonde hair, blue-eyed tiny angel with braces.

"Thank you for a fantastic lunch, sir."

"The pleasure was all mine." The Senator pulled out his cell phone and then removed himself from the table. "Please excuse me, I will be right back."

Two Secret Service men walked alongside the Senator as he disappeared to make his call. While the Senator was away, I took the liberty of making a private phone call myself. I called Khloe, and she told me that she had lost her job on the Hill. While she was explaining her situation, the Senator walked behind me and overheard my conversation. I hung up the phone and the Senator placed his hand on my shoulder.

"Would you like to tell me what that was all about?" the Senator asked.

"It's personal, sir."

"Sounds like you need a little assistance, Ms. Simms."

"We'll be fine, sir."

"It doesn't sound like you'll be fine to me."

"I've been through much worse than this. I'll be fine."

"Stop being so stubborn," the Senator smiled. "Remember, I'm a nice man."

The Senator took my hand in his and helped me to my feet. We left the restaurant and were headed back to the Capitol, when the Senator asked to use my cell phone. He used my phone to make a call to a man named Alexander.

"Alexander? This is the Senator. I need a spectacular living space by the end of the workday. I will also need a vehicle. Make it a luxury car," the Senator paused momentarily as Alexander absorbed the information. "Now listen closely, I want you to set up a personal bank account for one Ms. April Simms, and deposit the sum of one hundred thousand dollars. Contact Flora, she will give you Ms. Simms's personal information in her file. She is my new page. And yes, make sure that your name registers as her donor."

The Senator ended his call and handed my cell phone back to me. He then made another phone call to Alexander on his cell phone. He was using terms and names that were totally unfamiliar to me. Once he finished the second call to Alexander, he did not say another word until we arrived at the Capitol Building.

"This is my stop," the Senator talked to me as he waited for Maize to come around to open his door. "You won't be getting out here, Ms. Simms. You have business to tend to. My driver has instructions to take you to your new living accommodations. There you will find a vehicle registered in your name. Understood?"

"No, I...I don't understand, sir."

"You will." the Senator started to exit the car.

"Can my sister Khloe stay with me, sir?"

"I don't think that would be a good idea, Ms. Simms."

"Why not?"

"Hmm, perhaps it is time that you learn to be independent," the Senator stepped out of the car and then peeked back inside. "Enjoy the rest of your day, Ms. Simms."

Maize drove me to the district of Georgetown. Georgetown is a historic neighborhood located in the Northwest section of Washington D.C., along the Potomac River. It has old buildings, old streets and old money. And at that point, it had me.

Maize pulled in front of a row of very upscale condominiums. He stopped the car, and I was cognizant enough to sit still until he opened the door. I waited, but he did not come. I was not sure if I was following proper protocol, so I sat and contemplated my options. Do I sit until Maize opens my door? Does he only open the door for the Senator, and I am on my own? I knocked on the privacy window to inquire for clarity. Maize rolled the window down and looked at me through the rearview mirror. In a very deep, deep voice he spoke, "Ma'am?"

"I'm a little confused on whether or not I should be getting out, or should I...," I put my hands in the air in confusion. "What exactly are we doing right now?"

"We are waiting for the keys to your home, ma'am."

"My home? What home?" I asked. "Mr. Maize, can you please tell me what's going on? Why is the Senator buying me a home?"

"I'm sorry, ma'am, but I am not at liberty to discuss personal or private information of the Senator to anyone."

"This is kind of like my business, too. I just want to know what's going on."

"I understand, ma'am."

Maize slowly rolled up the partition. We sat for a few more minutes until a car quickly zoomed by and parked in front of our car. Maize stepped out of the car and walked around to my door. He opened the door and without saying a word, he took my hand and helped me out of the car. He silently stood next to me. Meanwhile, a woman rushed out of the car, parked in front of us, and apologetically shook my hand.

"I'm Charlotte, and I am so sorry I'm late, Ms. Simms. But when I received the call from Alexander, I was way across town and I had to rush through traffic to get here," Charlotte handed me a set of keys. "Here are your keys, and if you'll follow me, I'll show you your new home. I'm not sure if you're a condo person or not, but I thought this townhouse would be wonderful for you."

My first thought was, "How do you know what I like?" My second thought was, "Thank you for knowing what I like!" I followed Charlotte towards a beautiful red brick two-story townhouse. I unlocked the door, and then realized I was walking through the front door of my very own home. A week prior, I was a broke, unemployed, college student sleeping in a cheap motel. Standing in the foyer of my townhouse, I felt like I was living a dream. A dream that I did not deserve.

I probably should have refused the Senator's generosity, but everything was moving so fast that I did not feel I was in control of the situation. I could not blame it on my youth or inexperience, because I knew that nothing was for free. Everything had a cost, and eventually I would have to pay.

"Oh my, God! This place is gorgeous," my jaw dropped to the floor in amazement. "This place is absolutely incredible!"

We walked from room to room, and Charlotte explained in detail the features of each room. "As you can see, you have a lovely three-thousand square feet, four bedroom, three-and-a-half bath luxurious townhouse. You have immaculate hardwood floors, two fireplaces, gourmet eat-in kitchen with stainless steel appliances and granite countertops. Do you approve?"

"Do I approve?" I asked ecstatically. "Of course, I approve!"

"If you would like to go back out to your car, we can sign all of the documents now, and this home is yours."

I followed Charlotte as she led me back outside. "Excuse me, Charlotte, how long is the lease?"

"Indefinite, Ms. Simms," Charlotte smiled.

We sat in the back of the limo, and we signed each document. The entire situation seemed surreal to me, but for Charlotte it seemed business as usual. I sensed nervousness from Charlotte that if I was not satisfied with the property, she would undergo some form of repercussion or reprimand. Needless to say, I was in seventh heaven.

"Charlotte, may I ask you a question?"

"Sure. Ask me anything?"

"Why is the Senator buying me a house?"

"Excuse me?" Charlotte seemed unprepared for my question.

"I asked you, 'Why is a United States Senator buying me a home?'"

"Renting, Ms. Simms, renting," Charlotte smiled. "Actually…I am sorry, Ms. Simms, but I'm not at liberty to divulge any personal or private information about the Senator. I received a call from Alexander, and when Alexander calls, people move."

"I don't understand this. Why is everybody helping me?" I sighed. "A nobody!"

"Everybody is somebody, Ms. Simms," Charlotte opened the door and stepped outside. "Enjoy your new home."

"Thank you very much, Charlotte," I waited for Charlotte to close the door and then I screamed in frustration, "UGH!"

Maize opened the door and extended his hand, "Can you please follow me, ma'am?"

"Oh, OK."

Maize helped me out of the car, and I followed him to the garage of my new home. He raised the garage door, and there was a shiny brand-new red Ford Mustang with the sticker still on the window.

"Your new automobile, ma'am," Maize handed me the keys to the car.

"This is my car?"

"Yes, it is, ma'am."

"Wow! Is it a lease? Rental?"

"Yes, it is a lease," Maize smiled, "or a rental."

"You seem cool, Maize, now tell me," I pleaded for understanding. "Please tell me, why is this happening to me?"

"I'm not at liberty to…"

"I know! I know! You're not at liberty to discuss anything…blah, blah, blah!"

"Enjoy your automobile, ma'am."

"Right," I said sarcastically as I left Maize standing in the driveway.

That night, I had dream after dream about the Senator. He was consuming my mind. I went from admiring the man to being obsessively head-over-heels for the man. There was no explanation for my feelings. The fact that he used his influence to rent me a house and a car and made my bank account larger than I could imagine, should not in return influence my feelings of affection…but it did.

I invited Khloe to come for a visit, but at first, she was very apprehensive. After begging and pleading for a while, she gave in and agreed to come over. I was anxious to show her my new home. Not to show off, but to invite her and Kiera to come and live with me. I didn't really care what the Senator said. Khloe had done too much for me to turn my back on her in her time of need.

"How do you like our place, Khloe?" I asked.

"This is not our place, it's your place," Khloe answered. "The Senator rented this place for you, not me."

"I don't care what the Senator says, this place is all of ours!"

"It doesn't work like that, April."

"What do you mean? I signed my name on the lease. I can…"

"This is not Atlanta, April!" Khloe interrupted. "Things work differently here. You don't get something for nothing. The Senator is not just a nice man who wants to help you. He wants something in return."

"Something like what?"

"Don't be naïve, April."

"I'm not naïve. I'm asking."

"Look at this place." Khloe looks around with her hands in the air. "The Senator doesn't know you from anyone, and he all of sudden finds the generosity to rent you a house. Not a small apartment! A big ass house!"

"He's from Georgia, and…"

"Georgia ain't got shit to do with this, April. You know why he rented this place. The man is placing you in his own private box so that he can come play with you any time that he wants."

"Oh, I get it. You're upset because the Senator is giving me attention and not you."

"Have you lost your entire mind?" Khloe shouted. "I don't give a good gotdam about the Senator giving you attention. I'm trying to warn your stupid ass about what this man is trying to do to you."

"I'm just saying," I paused momentarily and then continued to talk, "we have an opportunity to live rent-free indefinitely and you tripping like we are prostituting or something."

"April, do you think that you are the only intern the Senator has offered gifts? No. You are just one of many."

"Are you one of them?"

Khloe looked at me and then paused before she spoke. She paced back and forth biting her lip, thinking of the proper response. "Look April, the Senator offered me an extravagant place to live, money, and all of that. But I said no. That's why I'm struggling to pay my bills and my rent. But I'd rather struggle on my own than to be indebted to anyone for giving me something that I didn't earn."

"Is that why the Senator doesn't want you to live here with me?"

"Yup. And that's why he fired me. I told him that you were hands off. The next thing I know, I got a pink slip."

"Oh shit," I said nervously. "What should I do, Khloe?"

"I don't have to tell you what to do with this one. Daddy has taught you right from wrong, just like he taught me. But whatever you decide, make sure you take care of yourself because I'm about to head back to the ATL."

"You can't do that. I need you."

"Not anymore, little sister. You have to deal with this one on your own. So, I'll leave you to your little castle," Khloe starts to head towards the door. "But if you ever need me, call me and I'm here. OK?

"OK." I said, holding back tears.

"How are you going to get back and forth to work? I can leave my car and use one of Daddy's until you get transportation."

"The Senator kind of rented me a car, too."

"Damn," Khloe chuckled, "the cheap bastard didn't even offer me a bus pass."

We both laughed.

"Thank you, Khloe."

"Be careful, April."

"I will."

Khloe waved goodbye and then walked out of the door.

I went to work the next morning, hoping to talk to the Senator. I wanted to tell him that I appreciated his generosity, but that I could not accept his gifts. However, he did not come into the office that day. In his absence, I found myself daydreaming about him the remainder of the day. I longed for the sound of his voice. I wanted to smell him. I needed to be in his presence. I felt like a teenage girl with a crush on a teenage boy. I wanted to lie in bed and talk to him all day. Instead, I had to work eight long hours with a green-eyed monster named Flora.

"Did you sharpen all of the pencils?" Flora asked.

"Yes, I did," I replied.

"Did you organize all of the ink pens by colors?"

"Yes, I did."

"Did you stack all of the empty manila folders in my desk?"

"Yes, I did."

"Good, now I need you to start calling the Senator's constituents."

"For what, Flora?"

"Fundraising."

"Really?" Flora and I both knew I could be much more valuable to the Senator than doing elementary assignments and making fundraising phone calls. "Fundraising phone calls, Flora?"

"Yes, that's what pages do."

"Fine."

I realized that if I was going to be successful in my endeavor to get through to the Senator, I would have to shift Flora over to my side or remove her altogether. I was convinced that she had feelings for the Senator. In order for her to feel comfortable with me, she was going to have to feel comfortable with knowing there was no romantic involvement between the Senator and me.

"Flora?"

"Yes, April?"

"Can we talk?" I approached her cautiously. "You know, girl to girl?"

"About what?"

"I'm getting negative vibes from you and I don't really know why."

"Really?" Flora faced me with a stern frown on her face. "You seriously don't know why?"

"No, I don't."

"Let me tell you why, April" Flora sighed heavily. "I have been working for the Senator for twenty-five years. I came to Washington with him from Georgia. We grew up together! We were childhood sweethearts. But I was never good enough. I wasn't good enough when I went to public high school and he started to date the debutante girls from private schools! I wasn't good enough when I went to a state college and he dated beauty

254

queens! I wasn't good enough when I went to work as a receptionist, and he married the beautiful blonde hair, blue-eyed, skinny daughter of a multi-millionaire! I was never good enough for him to love, April. But I was always good enough to work for him."

"I…I didn't know that," I felt sorry for Flora. "Are you in love with him?"

"I'm not even sure anymore. I know I was once, but now I think I've been loving him for so long it's just a part of who I am. I never married. I never had children, because I thought one day that he would open his eyes and see that I was the woman he should have married. Year after year! Child after child! Parker, Madison and then Autumn. I attended all of the baby showers, all of the christenings, all of the graduations! Everything! I left my life behind and now it's too late for me to go back and retrieve it."

"Does the Senator know how you feel about him, Flora?"

"No. And he never will."

"Why not?" I asked. "Don't you think he should know?"

"Oh my, April," Flora shook her head. "I look at that man when he looks at his wife. When he looks at her, he sees love, security and home. I also look at him when he looks at you. When he looks at you, he sees stimulation, sexiness and youth. When he looks at me, all that he sees is friendship, loyalty and subordination. But not the cohabitation of us living together in our own home. With me, he sees the familiarity of his roots in Georgia"

"I'm really trying to appreciate why you would commit your entire life to a man who doesn't love you back, Flora."

"It didn't start off that way. And I certainly didn't know it was going to end up this way. I thought if I stuck by his side, he would see me like he saw other women," Flora began to cry, which made me start to cry. "I wanted him to see love when he looked at me, but he never did, April. He never did."

"Flora, I mean this. I really and truly wish you luck working for this man. You're a beautiful, wonderful woman that I respect. You have no idea what you have taught me today, and I will forever be grateful. I, uh, I'm getting ready to go home now."

"What time will you be in tomorrow, April, because we have to…"

"No…you don't understand. I'm going home to my family in Atlanta. Take care."

I walked out of that office feeling ten feet tall. I didn't even bother to pick up my clothes or any of my property. I went straight to the airport and waited for the next flight headed to Atlanta. My life in Washington D.C. was short-lived, but long enough for me to grow into a woman. Although I will always appreciate my experience in Washington D.C., I never want to put myself in a compromising position like that again.

When that plane went airborne, I looked back on my life. I was born with HIV. I was abandoned as a child. I was raised by the state. I had hypertension, diabetes and bronchitis, and I survived it all. People tend to think that it takes blood to make you a family, but in reality, all that it takes is love. For all of the trials and tribulations that I have suffered, I wouldn't change a thing if it meant that I might not have ended up with the family that God has given me.

CHAPTER TWELVE

The Finale...

W hat a story," Dr. Turner said. "So, this scumbag that you worked for was the Senator from Georgia?"

"Yes."

"That bastard probably had no concern about his wife."

"If he did, he never showed it."

"Did you know his wife? Or, did you ever meet her?"

"No. I wasn't there that long. I never even saw a photo of her."

"But you knew he was married?"

"Yes, I did."

"Interesting," Dr. Turner said. "Well, our session is over, but I would like to speak with you and your sisters next week. Without dad."

"OK, I'll check with them but that shouldn't be a problem."

"Great. See you next week."

—

All three of my daughters had visited Dr. Turner for therapy. I had one more visit with Dr. Turner, and after all of these years, we would say goodbye. I felt that she had helped me to resolve issues within myself. However, since I wasn't privy to the information that my daughters provided to Dr. Turner, I was still uncertain of what part I had played in the emotional dysfunction of their lives.

When I arrived at Dr. Turner's office, she looked worse off than my previous visit. Something was wrong. I didn't want to appear as if I was concerned, but in reality, I was. I entered Dr. Turner's office sad, because we were saying goodbye. I would leave Dr. Turner's office wondering if she would survive the day.

"Are you," I paused, "is everything, OK, Dr. Turner?"

"It will be after today."

"Maybe we should move my session to another day?"

"No, today is fine."

"OK, well, I guess that's good to know."

"After five years of therapy, where do you find yourself today in comparison to where you were when you arrived?"

"I feel mentally healthy. I feel as if there are no more questions in my head about who I am. I know who I am."

"Great," Dr. Turner nodded and smiled. "You've made tremendous strides in your ability to assess emotional triggers and confront them and not allow them to remain dormant."

"Thank you. I realize now, that before I came to you, I had serious issues with expressing myself. But now, it doesn't seem to be an issue at all. My job. Strangers. I just have a better sense of relating to people now."

"What about your communication with your daughters?"

"I open up with my daughters, as well, and they open up to me. In my opinion, our level of communication is as good as it can be, but I still wonder how my daughters feel about me. I know they love me. But I don't know if they blame me for some of their emotional baggage, being that I wasn't around as much as I could have been when they were young."

"I don't think your daughters have any negative thought, or thoughts, on you not being around when they were young."

"Is that what they told you, Dr. Turner?"

"I am not at liberty to discuss what they actually told me; however, I can say that your daughters appear to be very secure with their relationships and the positive impact you have had in their lives."

"Thank you, Dr. Turner. That makes me feel a lot better, knowing that."

Suddenly, Dr. Turner's attitude seemed to change, "I would like to ask you a question, Mr. Simms."

"OK?" I asked curiously.

"Do you believe in infidelity?"

I was surprised by Dr. Turner's question, because it didn't coincide with our current conversation nor any previous conversations we have had.

"Yes. I haven't always subscribed to living a life of fidelity, but I have always believed that if you are in a monogamous relationship, you should be monogamous."

"How would you describe yourself in a relationship, Mr. Simms?"

"Now? Well, I'm faithful. Loyal. Respectful. Unselfish…"

"Have you ever been cheated on, Mr. Simms?" Dr. Turner interrupted me.

"Yes, I have."

"Were you married?"

"Yes, I was."

"Kids? House? Cars?"

"Yes."

"Did you stay with her after the affair?"

"Noooooo! Hell no! I left her."

"How did the affair make you feel, Mr. Simms?"

"I was hurt," I paused to reminisce on the pain I felt at that time. "I was embarrassed. I felt betrayed. I mean, I felt sick to my stomach."

"Did you want to hurt her?" I was stunned by Dr. Turner's direct and emotionless questioning. "Maybe even kill her?"

"I was angry. Very angry! But I didn't want to hurt her. Had she accidentally gotten run over by a bus, I can't say that I would have mourned her, though," I chuckled.

Dr. Turner looked at me, completely devoid of emotion, and said, "When people cheat and hurt others, they deserve whatever they get. To me, they deserve death."

"Don't you think that's a bit much, Dr. Turner?"

"No, I think that's karma, Mr. Simms."

"Are you sure there's nothing wrong, Dr. Turner?"

"Positive."

"Forgive me, I hate to be redundant, but you're acting very peculiar today."

Dr. Turner ignored me and continued with her questions, "How do you feel your absence affected your daughters' perspective on how they relate to men in a romantic scenario? Morally and ethically speaking, that is."

"Morally and ethically speaking? What do you mean?"

"When it comes to men, are they promiscuous? Licentious? Whores?"

"Whores? Are you OK, Dr. Turner?"

"Why do you keep asking me that, Mr. Simms?" Dr. Turner seemed annoyed.

"Because your questions are becoming unprofessional and inappropriate. They are certainly not the type of questions you have typically asked me. As a matter of fact, I am not understanding what's going in this session at all."

"I'm just showing you that there is a thin line between sanity and insanity, Mr. Simms," Dr. Turner smiled and then stopped abruptly. "You see, I talk to people every day about their problems and never does anyone ask about mine."

"You're mistaken, because I've asked about your welfare several times in this conversation, Dr. Turner."

"Only because my behavior is affecting your welfare, Mr. Simms. Not because you care. No one cares about Dr. Turner. So long as I am here to hear and cure everyone else's problem, everyone else is happy."

"I don't mean to sound rude or insensitive, but isn't it your job to listen to us?'

"Of course, you would say and think that. You're a man."

"I don't understand what my gender has to do with this conversation, Dr. Turner."

"Men are selfish, stupid, egotistical, narcissistic pigs. That's what your gender has to do with it," Dr. Turner snarled. "You're a gotdam man!"

"OK!" Enough was enough! Dr. Turner was definitely not Dr. Turner. "I see that you're having a bad day, so how about we end our session here? I am very disappointed that we had to end our therapy this way after all of these years, but it is what it is. It has been a pleasure, and I thank you for all of your assistance, Dr. Turner."

"Go ahead! Leave! Get the hell out!"

I walked to the door and grabbed the doorknob. I looked back to tell Dr. Turner goodbye, but her head was down, and she was crying hysterically. I walked out and slowly closed the door behind me. To try to explain my thoughts at that moment would be an insult to my comprehensive ability to convey myself. Afterwards, I thought that Dr. Turner had had a nervous breakdown right in front of me. She had clearly had a meltdown of gargantuan proportions.

As I walked to my car, I tried to call the girls and tell them about my unusual session with Dr. Turner, but neither of them answered their phones. I sat in my car,

looking in my mirror staring at myself, still perplexed as to what the hell just happened in that office. I put the key in the ignition and started my car. I started to drive in reverse and noticed a couple walking behind my rear bumper, so I slammed on the brakes and stopped.

The man grabbed the woman by the arm to prevent her from walking further in front of me. As she laid her head on his chest and sighed, another woman walked past from the opposite direction. The woman was magnificently beautiful. The man's eyes watched her approach and then wandered in her direction as she continued past. The man's head was turned as much as his flexibility would allow. The woman noticed the man's eyes following the other woman, and she playfully punched him in the chest. He chuckled, and then kissed her apologetically. I shook my head and then I smiled. Watching them made me think of Dr. Turner's comments in her office about men and infidelity. My phone rang and it was Khloe.

"Hey, baby?" I said, as I answered.

"What you doing, Daddy?" Khloe asked.

"Leaving Dr. Turner's office."

"Oh really? We're in her building now."

"I didn't know you all were meeting with Dr. Turner today."

"It's a sisters' session, so she thought it would be best if we just did this one as sisters."

"You may have to postpone that meeting."

"Why do you say that?"

"Well our therapist is having a very bad day."

"What happened?" Khloe asked.

"I think our therapist needs a therapist, and quick."

"We just spoke to her and she seemed fine to us."

"Put him on speaker, Khloe," Kiera said.

Khloe put me on speaker so that April and Kiera could hear me.

"Daddy, are you jealous that we stole your therapist?" April asked.

"Not at all. I'm just warning you girls that Dr. Turner is not herself today. But maybe I did something to set her off. Or maybe she was having some type of emotional reaction to this being our last meeting."

"Aren't we the narcissist?" Khloe joked.

"I'm just saying, girls. Prepare yourself. There's no telling what you're going to get in there. OK?"

"OK, Daddy," Kiera said. "We ready for anything. This kind of fun."

"OK, Daddy, we're about to get on the elevator and my phone may go out, so I'm about to hang up. We'll tell you how it went when we get out."

"OK," I said. "Bye, girls."

"Bye, Daddy!" the girls say in unison.

The girls thought the phone was disconnected and then they started to talk amongst themselves. I heard April jokingly say, "Now when Dr. Turner brings up the Senator, we're going to both act like we didn't do nothing with him, OK?"

Like any father, hearing that comment would make him pause, but for me--I had a sudden feeling of panic. The smile that was on my face quickly turned into a mask of horror.

"SHIT!" I screamed and slammed on my brakes.

—

When my daughters entered the office, Dr. Turner was sitting calmly with her hair strewn all over her head. Her eyes had mascara running from her eyes to her cheeks. The girls immediately noticed Dr. Turner's appearance and looked at one another with concern.

"Good afternoon, girls," Dr. Turner said with a friendly smile, followed by an ominous frown.

"Hey," Kiera said.

"Good afternoon, Dr. Turner," April smiled and waved. Dr. Turner did not reciprocate her warm greeting.

"Good afternoon," Khloe said as she sat between the other two sisters.

"When your father entered my office for his first session, he was afraid that his absence in your lives had caused you all to suffer some form of mental illness. He told me that the salt from your tears often rained down upon his heart, and that he wanted to purify your tears and rectify his past. From my analysis, your father is a very loving, caring and unselfish man who loves all three of you immeasurably." Dr. Turner paused and then continued. "However, I would like to add that there is a thin line between sanity and insanity. Sometimes, we can barely notice when which is which. For example, yesterday, I was a mentally healthy woman with a healthy and loving family. My psychological and emotional well-being was sound and intact. Today, I would diagnose myself with suffering from a severe and damaging mental illness. I am not stable. My mind is battling itself between sanity and insanity."

Khloe, April and Kiera look at one another with confusion.

"I'm not sure we understand what you're talking about," Khloe said.

"You see, I know who you are, but neither of you know who I am. I don't know if you're stupid or just lazy thinkers," Dr. Turner replied.

"Daddy was right, this lady acting crazy, y'all," Kiera said nervously.

"What the hell are you talking about?" Khloe asked impatiently.

"Shut the hell up! I ask the questions in here. Now…" Dr. Turner pulls out a gun and points it at the sisters. "One of you bitches slept with my husband and that completely ruined my life. So since you have destroyed my family, I feel it's only fair if I destroy yours. Today, we will all die.

"Oh, my God! You're the wife!" April shouted.

Dr. Turner nervously waves the gun aimlessly in the air. She grips the trigger and then points it back and forth at all three of the girls.

"So, which of you dirty little whores want to die first?" Dr. Turner frowns sinisterly. "How about I start with the oldest and work my way down, huh?"

Khloe, April and Kiera have scared looks on their faces.

"Look, this gotta' be a misunderstanding or something. You got us mixed up with somebody else."

"No, I have the right people who hurt my family, and I am about to settle the score."

"I don't know what you need to settle, but it ain't with me. I don't even like men. So, can I go?" Kiera pleaded.

"Really, Kiera?" Khloe snapped.

"Why everybody gotta' die?" Kiera cried.

"Look, I slept with the Senator, so I'll deal with the consequences," April looked at Khloe and Kiera and said, "Let my sisters go."

"Aww, look at you willing to die for the clan," Dr. Turner said sarcastically, "My office. My rules. You destroyed my entire family. Now I'm going to destroy your entire family."

Khloe grabs Kiera and April's hands, "You may kill us. But you can never destroy us or our family, you crazy bitch!"

"Is that right?" Dr. Turner holds the gun in the air, "Die!"

Khloe, April and Kiera stand, clutching each other's arms and prepare for Dr. Turner to fire the weapon. Dr. Turner walks from behind her desk and aims the gun at Khloe. Khloe pushes April and Kiera behind her. When Dr. Turner puts her finger on the trigger, I rushed through the door, catching her off guard. I saw the gun in her hand, pointed at my daughters. Although I was seeing it with my own eyes, I still couldn't believe it. It was surreal.

"What the hell are you doing?" I shouted.

"DADDY!" the girls screamed in unison.

"Mr. Simms?" Dr. Turner was surprised. "I tried to spare you the same fate as your homewrecking daughters but...like always, here you are being the good Daddy."

I positioned myself between Dr. Turner and the girls. "Things are not as bad as they seem. Put down the gun."

"You don't know what my life is like, Mr. Simms. My husband is gone."

"You're right, you're right," I tried to alleviate the tension by agreeing with Dr. Turner. "I don't know. But what I do know is, wherever he is, he is not with one of my girls. I can guarantee you that."

"Ask them!" Dr. Turner gestures with her gun for me to ask my girls about her husband. "Ask your precious girls about my husband?"

Without taking my eyes off of Dr. Turner, I asked my girls about the Senator, "What uh, what's she talking about, girls?"

"I had an affair with her husband, Daddy. But it was way before we met her," Khloe said.

"It doesn't matter! You knew he was married!" Dr. Turner shouted.

"He told me he was getting a divorce! How did I know he was lying? His wife lived in Georgia! He lived in Washington!" Khloe was crying as she was pleading for forgiveness from Dr. Turner, me, and herself.

"You knew exactly what you were doing," Dr. Turner said.

"Look!" I shouted. "She's sorry. I'm sorry. But we need to relax and think about what's happening right now."

"There's nothing to think about. It's over. My marriage. My family. My life. It's over."

"Don't talk like that. You've helped so many people. So many people. You're the best at this. And like you said earlier, everybody wants you to help them and nobody wants to help you. Well, I'm here. I'm here to help you."

"You're here to help your whores!"

"No! No!" I shook my head and then nodded, "Yes, I am, but I'm here to help you, too."

"It's too late. You can't help me, Mr. Simms."

"I can, if you can just help me, to help you. I need you. I need you to help me. I want all of us to walk out that door...together."

"I'm sorry." Dr. Turner wiped her eyes with the hand that was holding the gun and then she shook her head, no. "We're not leaving. None of us are."

"Well, let my daughters go and you and I can stay here and talk. We can talk as long as you want. For as long as it takes."

"They are the ones who did this to me! They are going to die with me!" Dr. Turner shouted.

"No, they're not. You're not going to hurt them. You wanna' know why? Because you know they're not responsible for your husband. Your husband is responsible for hurting you. Come on, you know this. Still, it's never too late," I tried to switch my negotiation tactic to reinforcing the possibility that Dr. Turner's marriage could be saved. And I received the shock of my life. "Maybe if you all talked, get counseling, who knows? Maybe you can salvage your marriage."

"It's too late."

"Only if you think it's too late. You all have a history. You have children. It's never too...," Dr. Turner yelled at me while I was in mid-sentence.

"IT'S TOO GOTDAM LATE!"

"OK! OK! OK! Calm down," While Dr. Turner was distracted with her frustration, I started to move slowly towards the door.

The Salt From Their Tears
As I continued to talk, I began to slowly push my daughters

towards the door, too. "I'm just looking at things from all angles."

Finally, the girls were at the door, and I stood between them and Dr. Turner. Khloe inconspicuously reached for the doorknob, as Dr. Turner continued to talk to me.

"What kind of a person can save everyone but herself?"

"This is not your fault, Dr. Turner," I said. "Don't go blaming yourself. It's not your fault! It's not the girls' fault! The Senator did this, and he has to fix it."

"It's too late!" Dr. Turner shouted again.

I looked back at Khloe and she looked at me. I nodded, cluing her to get ready to make her move. I was nervous. The girls were scared. I had my weapon inside the waist of my pants, so I would have to snatch my pistol out simultaneously as the girls ran outside. I didn't want to hurt Dr. Turner, as I had grown quite fond of her. She had helped me when I needed help most, and I was indebted to her. But we were at a crossroad of the survival of the fittest, and it was either Dr. Turner or my girls.

"Why is it too late?" I tried one more attempt to reason with her.

I had no more negotiation tactics. No more pleading. No more answers. It was time for me to get my daughters out of that potentially deadly situation. I didn't care what happened to me. I didn't want to die, but if it meant saving my daughters, I was willing to die in an instant. I just wanted them safe.

Time was up! The moment of truth had arrived. I looked over to Khloe, and then I looked into the eyes of Kiera and April. I could see and feel their fear through the tears flowing from all of their eyes. The salt from their tears began to rain down upon my heart, and I realized that this was the moment that I would purify those tears and rectify my past. My life for their lives. My mind was swirling. My heart was racing. As I reached for my weapon, Dr. Turner replied to my question.

"He's dead," Dr. Turner mumbled.

I stopped motioning for my weapon, and the girls stopped reaching for the door, as we tried to process what we had just heard.

"What?" I said in disbelief.

"It's too late because he's dead."

"What…what are you saying?"

"He's gone," Dr. Turner started to raise her gun and I reached for mine. "My husband is dead. I killed him."

"I beg you, please, put that weapon down and let's talk this out!"

"It's too late," Dr. Turner lowered her gun and I began to relax, but it was only for a moment.

Suddenly, Dr. Turner raised her gun, which forced me once again to pull my weapon. Dr. Turner pointed her gun at me, and I pointed my gun at her, while pushing my girls out of the door. She had a clear shot at my chest, but instead of firing, she spread a sad grin across her face and then continued to raise the gun to the side of her head.

"NOOOOOOOOOOOO!" I screamed, as she pulled the trigger. Dr. Turner's body collapsed to the floor, and I ran to her side and screamed to the top of my lungs, "HELLLLLLLLLLLP! Karen? Karen? Please?"

—

After the shooting of Dr. Turner, I made a point to speak with each of my children separately and confidentially. They

The Salt From Their Tears

me everything they had revealed to Dr. Turner. My heart was broken but with the truth I could wipe the salt from their tears. I decided we should talk as family and I could tell my daughters just how much I loved them. I took the girls to lunch at a fancy restaurant in Buckhead. I did not give them a reason. I just asked them to meet me so that we could talk. They were nervous because we just don't do random meals in Buckhead. We sat down and I looked at them and smiled.

"Is everything alright, Daddy?" Khloe asked.

"Yes, sweetheart."

"Whoo! Thank God," Khloe sighed.

"Daddy you tryin' to give us a heart attack!" Kiera fans herself.

"Can't a father take his daughter to lunch?"

"I'm sorry, Daddy. Yes, a father can take his daughter to lunch. Thank you for thinking of me," Khloe said.

"Since you're the oldest, I'll start with you, Khloe," I said. "I want to apologize for everything that happened to you. I know I may not deserve it, but I hope someday that you can forgive me. I know how difficult it may be because I am having a hard time forgiving myself. Despite everything that happened to you, you grew up to be a very bright, respectful and beautiful young lady. You always knew that whatever you needed to do, just do it no matter what with no excuses. You handle your business, Khloe. You are truly a soldier. I remember times when you would study all night long to make sure you aced your exams. I didn't have to stay on you about anything because you were always on it.

"I don't know where you developed those discipline and attention to details traits, but you certainly didn't get them from me. Even as a teenager, you came here to live with me so that I could take care of you, but you helped me get myself together.

You've helped your younger sisters stay on task and take responsibility for their actions far beyond the scope of a big sister. You work hard and don't make excuses. Your senior year, you wanted to be independent, so you got you a job, worked hard, and bought yourself a car. You would drive yourself to school and have perfect attendance.

"You won Homecoming Queen and I'm not just saying this because you're my daughter, but none of those other girls had a chance. You researched and picked out the college you wanted to attend. You did it all by yourself. But I do thank you for including me in some of the experience beyond my wallet," I chuckle and kiss Khloe on the cheek. "What did you say, 'Daddy, okay, which college should I attend, Howard, Spelman or Clark-Atlanta?'" I only got in your way. But seriously, sweetheart, everybody has sins and secrets. From now on, we won't. I want you to feel comfortable telling me anything. You're grown but I'm still daddy and you never have to go through anything alone. Understand?"

"Oh my, God, Daddy, what you doing? You're going to make me cry." Khloe is crying. I can't believe you remember all of that stuff. I love you so much!"

Khloe hugged me and gave me a big kiss.

"April?" I smiled. "Well, sweetheart, I just wanted to let you know that, I love you. And even though you may not have been born to me biologically, I can't love you anymore than I do. Understand?"

"I love you, too, Daddy."

"When I received the call from the adoption agency in LA telling me that I could sign the final paperwork and you could come to Atlanta, I was nervous. No, I was scared, and I was uncertain as to how this could work. When I brought you home with me, you were attached to a heart monitor. I was trained on how to use it. That alarm would sound off nearly every hour because you had a heart murmur and it would palpitate irregularly. Sometime, when you positioned yourself awkwardly in your bed, man, that alarm would scream. I was always on edge when it came to you because I was afraid that the beautiful soul that lives inside of you would never get the opportunity to shine itself on the world. God doesn't make mistakes but I'm glad he fixes things, like making me your father. From this day forward, I don't ever want us to mention the word biological in reference to you and I being a father and daughter. OK?"

"Never again, Daddy. Never!" April wiped her eyes. You are my hero."

"No, baby, you are my hero," I said. "I love you."

"I love you, too, Daddy." April hugged and kissed me.

"And then there's you," I said as I looked at Kiera.

"Oh, shit. I'mma 'boutto break down and Daddy ain't even said nothin' yet."

"Stop cussin' in front of Daddy, lil' girl!" Khloe said.

"I'm sorry, Daddy. I got caught up," Kiera pleaded.

"It's OK, baby. Don't do it again, but it's OK," I said firmly. "When I look at you, Kiera, it's like looking in a mirror. Even when you were a baby, you copied everything that I did. When you grew older you would literally walk in my footsteps trying to mimic me. You would constantly say that you wanted to grow up to be me. I was amazed that my beautiful child wanted to be me. Now imagine my reaction when you finally came out and told me that you like girls. I pretended to be understanding, thoughtful and caring. But it was hard to understand why you were like you were and I initially I blamed myself. I thought

276

that

if I hadn't let you behave so much like me maybe you would have been straight, and I would have had a normal child.

"I tried to make you get involved in cheerleading, but you were so unhappy that I pulled you out. Then I tried to encourage you to date boys even though I thought you were too young. I compromised my own morals to try to get you to change yours. After I tried everything I could I decided to talk to you. You were still very young, so I didn't know if you were just going through a phase or if girls were your true sexual preference. You told me that you were proud and happy to like girls and you explained the LGBTQ letters. I still don't remember what they mean. To be totally honest, baby, after we talked, I cried that day because I finally realized that there was no turning you straight.

"But after seeing how strong and proud you were it made me all of my fears go away. I realized that it wasn't that you liked girls, I was afraid that your life would be painful and filled with bigotry and prejudice. Talking to you made me understand that I was one of the bigots. Then I used our discussion as an opportunity to listen to you and find out what you needed. As you grew into yourself, you became the most extraordinary, beautiful, and unique young lady I have ever met.

"I remember our first pride parade. You wore a t-shirt that read, 'I'm the queer daughter of a straight daddy.' Everybody laughed and made me feel welcome. Although you are the youngest of the bunch, you are my heartbeat."

"That's going to do it right there," Khloe said.

"Yeah, she's gonna blow," April laughed.

"Dad-deee!" Kiera sobbed and then stood up and ran around the table and hugged me from behind. She was so animated that my chair started tipping backwards.

"Baby, you're going to make daddy's chair tip over if you don't let me go," I said.

"I ain't never letting you, Daddy! Oh my, God! I love this man so much," Kiera cried.

"I wish you were a stud lesbian. Your emotional ass drives me nuts," Khloe said.

"Stop cussin' in front of Daddy, Khloe!" Kiera shouted, still hugging me from behind.

"Watch your mouth, Khloe Simmons," April added.

"Now ladies, I would like to tell you the purpose of our lunch date." I said.

"This wasn't it?" Kiera asked.

"Not quite. I documented all of my visits to Dr. Turner and I decided to turn them into memoirs. After Dr. Turner shot herself in her office, I was contacted by a publishing company and they want to write my story about my relationship with my daughters."

"Can I help write it?" Kiera asked.

"I already have an assistant and she is doing an excellent job," I looked at April and smiled.

"You knew Daddy was writing a book?" Khloe asked April.

"Yes, but he told me not to say anything until he was sure he was going to do it," April answered.

"Daddy, I wanna be an assistant, too," Kiera said.

"Girl, you can't even talk how in the hell you gon' help write a book?" Khloe joked.

"I can't stand yo' ass sometime," Kiera joked back.

"Anyway, y'all. Daddy will be having his first book signing in a couple of months so tell everybody you know because we want that place packed," April said.

"Look at my little sister handling business," Khloe said.

"Well can I at least introduce you at your book signing, Daddy?" Kiera asked.

"That's not a thing, Kiera," April said.

"It's not?" Kiera asked.

"Hell no!" Khloe snapped.

—

"Ladies and gentlemen, without further ado, I would like to introduce the best father a girl could ever have, my daddy, Andre Simms!" Kiera said as I approached the podium.

I was nervous because I wasn't expecting that many people. My daughters promised the house would be packed but it was standing room only. I held my book in my hand as I begin to talk to he audience.

"As a father, writing this book about the story of my daughters was a surreal process that inadvertently resulted in much needed therapy. I am forever grateful to have been blessed with such wonderful daughters, Khloe, April and Kiera. I appreciate their ongoing support in bringing our story to life. It is because of their efforts and encouragement that we have built a legacy that will withstand the test of time and that legacy is in good hands to be passed down to our posterity. I thank my children for allowing me to be their father and molding me into their dad.

"I would also like to dedicate this story to all of the fathers who have daughters, or have lost daughters, please know that the bond between a father and his daughter is invaluable. It is a special relationship where he is the first protector and provider and his example can set a standard for the rest of her life. To all the daughters who share that special bond with your father and are, 'Daddy's Girls,' enjoy every single second that you spend with him. For the daughters who have fathers and would love to establish a stronger bond with them, follow your heart and make plenty of special memories that will last forever.

"Proverbs 31:30-31 "Charm is deceitful, and beauty is vain, but a woman who fears the Lord is to be praised. Give her of the fruit of her hands, and let her works praise her in the gates." "I am the daughter of a King that is not moved by the world. For my God is with me and goes before me. I do not fear because I am His." Daughters are a beautiful blessing from the Lord. God's word is the main source for training a godly girl into a godly woman. Tell her about Christ. Encourage your daughter with the Bible so she can grow up to be a strong Christian woman. There is nothing ordinary about you. You all are the daughters of the King.

"When I wrote "The Salt from Their Tears" I was hoping that it affected people in a way where they could find a meaningful source of healing. My book is a story of emotional and mental illness. I hope that those of you who have read it found comfort in knowing that mental illness does not have to be an immovable obstacle that causes you to retreat to your homes or your minds. There is help. There is always help. I am living witness.

"Finally, I have a very special friend in the audience. She has helped me through some very confusing years. She taught me how to confront my emotions and deal with them rationally and practically. She also showed me that when anybody is capable of having a temporary moment of mental illness that could lead to permanent consequences. She is a fighter. She is the winner.

She is the epitome of strength. She is the prime example of mental health, mental illness and mental recovery. Um, I could go on and on and on with adjectives that wouldn't give her the justice she deserves so I will just have her stand so that we recognize her for all that she's done for me personally, and what she has done for the profession of mental health."

"Daddy, can I introduce her, please?" Kiera asked.

"Why not?" I smiled and stepped away from the podium.

"Ladies and gentlemen, can you all stand and please give a loud and proud applause to Doctor and our new Senator-elect, Karen Turner!"

"Good evening ladies and gentlemen. Because of our unique patient-doctor relationship, Mr. Simms asked me to write the foreword for his book. Then he asked me to read the foreword aloud here today. So here I am. I am Doctor Karen Turner and I was Mr. Simms therapist for nine years. Often times, we hear the term, mental illness. There is an equally significant, yet, contrasting term that has an opposite or diametrically antonymous meaning. It is called mental wellness. Mental wellness is defined as, a state of well-being in which the individual realizes his or her own abilities, and can cope with the normal stresses of life, can work productively and fruitfully, and is able to make a contribution to his or her community.

"After practicing family therapy for nearly thirty years, and counseling thousands of patients, the stress of my personal life took its toll on me when I could no longer ignore the numerous affairs that my husband had been having for decades. When I was confronted with my own truth and my own family crisis, I could not cope with it and I had a nervous breakdown in my office in front of my patients and I tried to take my life. Thank God Mr. Simms was there. He became a diversion and talked to me, about me, as I had talked to him, about him, for years.

"I was so mentally ill in that moment that I became delusional. I felt so much pain and anger that day that I thought I had killed my husband. Looking back, that doesn't seem like such a bad idea. Certainly, would have solved a lot of problems immediately,'" Dr. Turner joked. "As Mr. Simms talked to me that day, I realized I didn't really want to die. It was just too painful to live. While my mind was trapped between living or dying, the gun fired. I was fortunate that the bullet only ricocheted off of my head and into my desk. I was so traumatized by the reality that I had shot myself that I fainted. When I regained consciousness, I was surrounded by Mr. Simms and his three beautiful daughters. The girls were crying. They were crying for me. As they cried, I wiped their tears from their eyes. Then I realized, I was crying, too. For years I have been wiping the tears of my patients, my family, and my friends, but nobody was wiping mine. That day, as Khloe, April and Kiera sat over me, I wiped the salt from their tears... and they washed the salt from mine. I left my husband. I divorced him and receive alimony and child support. Then, this past November, I took his job and I became a United States Senator.

"What makes Mr. Simms' book so important to anyone and everyone is that, it is a story of family, communication, self-caring, healing and love. Because at some point in our lives, if you really love someone, there will come a time when we will all need to wash the Salt from Their Tears."